AF443869

ALTARS AND FOUNDATIONS

MESHACH I. ALFA, PhD

ALTARS AND FOUNDATIONS

HOW TO OBTAIN YOUR INHERITANCE THROUGH THE DIVINE JUSTICE SYSTEM OF GOD

MESHACH I. ALFA, PhD

ISBN 978-978-984-261-2

REVIEWS FOR THE BOOK

The reader will have moments of great illuminations that produces transformation and turning points in life's journey. Pastor Meshach has produced an enduring work that will help the Body of Christ, particularly in Africa, to shift to a Christocentric victory mentality rather than the present all sweat rumbling with defeated forces of darkness. I greatly recommend the appropriation of the invaluable nuggets of truth in this book.

Kennedy Obi
Chief Steward,
Ever-Increasing Glory Int'l Ministry Inc., Warri, Nigeria

In Altars and Foundations Dr Meshach Alfa brings the long desired balance on the subject of deliverance and the New Creation perspectives of the Christian theology, even though he doesn't mention deliverance as a subject. This exposition on altars and their effects is a must read for everyone who desires to break away from mediocrity and other forms of bondage. This book is a treasure and I urge every minister of the gospel to get a copy.

Kenneth Ikeokwu
Senior Pastor - The Advancement Church;
Convener: Love and Family Matters, Lagos, Nigeria

I have known Pastor Meshach Alfa as a Passionate and excellent teacher of the word right from our days at the Nigeria Christian Corpers Fellowship in Kano State, Nigeria, 2008.

The Book "Altars and Foundations" at a first glance, may appear to be on the same page with some long-standing and traditional teachings on the subject of "Altars & Foundations" but I promise you, same does not apply. Pastor Meshach writes from the lens of the finished works of Christ, showing us that while we do not deny the existence of Spiritual attacks, evil altars and foundations, the dynamics of the operations of Satan etc., that we (as believers) have a positional advantage as a result of the death, the burial, and the resurrection of Jesus Christ.

This Book, is a three-part Spiritual encyclopaedia that aims to communicate and bring to our understanding the totality of the truths in subjects like *Man & Altars, the dynamics of the heavenly court, the deceptive operations of Satan as the accuser and the subject of knowledge as a core basis for Christian living.* This Book is a generational asset and there is no doubt, billions of people around the world who will come in contact with this book will be blessed just as I have been.

Sam Agu Bruno.
Author, Life Is Spiritual;
Snr Pastor, Hopeway The-Bridge London.
August 2020.

This is a good book; filled with basic foundational teaching but backed with revelational insights and apt examples.

Professor Victor S. Dugga
Senior Elder, Enoch Centre, Lafia;
Dean, Faculty of Arts, Federal University Lafia, Nigeria

■■

It's a great piece! A good work. My friend, Pastor Meshach has given us a clear presentation of the truth of the gospel, bringing forth time-proven revelations that will enable the believer access his inheritance in Christ and rise above the vicissitudes of life. I recommend this book to every believer.

Prophet Jesse N. Jangfa
Lord of Hosts Harvests Ministry, Jos, Nigeria

■■

As a purpose and God-driven person myself, I'm blessed by this book. This book challenged me to rise to another dimension of my inheritance through the justice system of God. Altars and Foundations is a shifting change that all believers must read. The keys to obtaining our inheritance in God is the knowledge of God, the knowledge of our position in God and the knowledge of Satan's predicament through the finished work of Christ. Wow!

What this book will do for you is to open your mind to the multifaceted dimensions of God almighty. I love this. So, shutdown the fear, drop what you are doing right now and read it.

Thank you for the great work my dear friend Pastor Meshach I. Alfa, PhD.

Dr. Amos Thomas
President, Treasured Life Covenant Ministry, Chicago IL

A highly inspirational book. It will challenge you to rise up violently to claim all that is yours in Christ Jesus.

Rev'd Monday Omede
Minister in Charge, ECWA Goodnews, Wusasa, Zaria, Nigeria

This book succinctly and adequately reveal the actual experience of a believer in his/her earthly walk being a system under the control of the god of this world. Many have taken issues like this to the extreme, either utterly glorifying the works of the devil thus frustration the grace and power of Christ in us or denying the reality of evil altars and foundations. This book sets a balance by giving us clear biblical exegesis of the issue of foundations as it relates to the destiny of humanity.

Rev'd. Ajayi A. Stanley
Remnant Christian Network Auchi, Edo State, Nigeria

I thoroughly enjoyed the background style of the first part, where the author laid out the relevance of the knowledge of God that we must have in terms of specific attributes of God. This type of 'knowing that we know that we know Him, that is, this 'ginosko' of God as all that He is to us, creates an intimacy that propels us into the place of oneness with heaven. Following on from that, I was blessed by the clear outlining of our knowledge of ourselves in God. It is so crucial that we are able to see ourselves through the eyes of the Father in order that we can know who we are truly. And yes, we cannot truly know all that we are until we have grown in knowledge and intimate revelation of God. The more of Him we become intimate with, the more of ourselves He reveals to us. How awesome!

The author took me on a journey in part two on an exposition that began with the foundations of altars with such clear examples, and ended with the solution: Christ.

The writing style was easy to read, flowed from page to page; and the sections were organised as to allow the Spirit of God uncover these truths step by step to the reader. I have been truly refreshed by this.

In the times and seasons we are living through, it is crucial that we don't live unaware of our rights as believers or of the work we need to do to enforce the kingdom of heaven here on earth in our lives. A lack of knowledge of our legal and judicial spiritual rights as believers is costly. I pray that this book gets read far and wide and that it brings much needed clarity and victory to every life it touches. I am so proud of you. Honestly. Proud that I got to be part of your journey and your story. May the Lord continue to perfect His work in you now and always.

Pastor Ezinne Obi Oriaku
Psychological Wellbeing Practitioner,
Hertfordshire Partnership University NHS Foundation Trust,
99 Waverley Rd, St Albans AL3 5TQ, United Kingdom

The issues dealt with here are amazing and life transforming, in fact in my honest opinion trans-generationally impactful. Very rich in content and reveals depths of truths and mysteries that are pivotal for believers to reach maturity and experiential liberty.

Pastor Jacob Timothy Adeyinka
Itinerant Minister of the Gospel, Abuja, Nigeria

Everywhere you look today, our world is impoverished by the parasite of paucity, ravaged by ravens of rancour, plagued by counsels of cruelty, sickened by insatiable worms of war and want. Are you fed up with fruitless toil? Most of all these are sponsored by altars and foundations.

For the Lord is our Judge, the Lord is our Lawgiver, the Lord is our King; He will save us... Isa 33:22, the executive, Judiciary and Legislative dimensions of God are wound up in this peerless parcel. If you long for the stature that nurtures substance; search no farther. A glory-clad odyssey awaits you as you adventure through mouth-watering menu engraved within this sacred seal.

What are Altars and Foundations? Are there some undercover dynamics that engender or endanger the potency of this hallowed bureau? How can we approach the court room of heaven to overturn the effect of foundations? These are the cherished diminuendos that **Dr. Meshach I. Alfa** – himself a seasoned intercessor – underlines and expertly underscores in this top-notch Spirit-breathed thriller. This book, **ALTARS AND FOUNDATIONS**, couldn't be timelier, we live in a time when curses hover broodingly over our darkened and disfigured landscape, waiting for willing wards to shoulder the cloak of intercession and destroy the clarion anthem of satanic altars and foundations. Here, in your very hands is the oasis to end your drought and factor in you a fresh fountain to water the wells of weary souls and advance the frontiers of God's kingdom in the earth.

Engr. Dr. Ezekiel Oiganji
Vision Bearer, Rescue Team Network;
Lecturer, Department of Crop Production,
Faculty of Agriculture, University of Jos.

You will certainly enjoy more spiritual ventilation walking in these revealed truths.

Prophet Ezekiel Jesufunmi
Lead Pastor, The Potters' Family Church, The Potters'
Apostolic Ministries, Kaduna, Nigeria

We fight battles we didn't bargain for, we struggle unnecessarily, we work like an elephant but eat like an ant, when we are about to rise a force from somewhere will show up to pull us down. These are mysterious battles we must know how to fight and overcome. For both spiritual and physical growth in life please get this book. You can't remain the same after reading it

Apostle Blessed E. Wonders
Itinerant Minister of the Gospel, Enugu, Nigeria.

DEDICATION

...to the Father, whose love for us propelled Him to give His beloved Son as a propitiation for our sin, to Jesus Christ, who purchased us to God by His Blood, to the Holy Spirit, the Seal of our redemption and the Breath of my existence and to all families who through this book will walk in the reality of the new life in Christ!

ACKNOWLEDGEMENTS

The book you are holding in your hand is a product of many testimonies. While I am most grateful to the Almighty God for enabling me to bring forth this piece, I will like to appreciate all the people who through the years contributed immensely to my spiritual development. It might interest you to know that some of them read and commented on this project. Thank you for believing in me and contributing to my spiritual growth.

This project would not be possible without the understanding and support of my dear wife, Annie and my lovely children, Jedidiah, David and Michael. Thank you very much for your understanding and the sacrifice of our family time to see that this project is a success.

Time will not permit me to mention everyone by name but permit me to specially appreciate Rev'd, Prof. Emmy I. U. Idegu who took out time to write the Foreword, Prof. Victor S. Dugga, Pastor Kennedy Obi, Pastor Ken Ikeokwu, Rev'd Monday Omede, Prophet Ezekiel Jesufunmi, Apostle Gideon Odoma, Pastor Ezinne Obi Oriaku, Apostle Sam Bruno, Dr. Amos Thomas, Prophet Jesse Jangfa, Pastor Jakes Adeyinka and Pastor Stanley Ajayi whose constructive reviews greatly improved the message of this book. Thank you for your immense contributions.

Lastly, thank you to the production team for the excellent work.

FOREWORD

Writing books, both at the secular and spiritual spheres demands a lot of discipline, knowledge in the chosen area, conviction in the ideas being given out to the reader and above all, the readiness to share experience that can greatly assist the reader in refocusing, realigning and re-strategizing self for today and the future. Writing Christian books demands the greatest care, discipline, dedication, humility and willingness to go as He leads. I congratulate Pastor Dr Meshach Ileanwa Alfa for bringing out for the Christian consumption, another highly guided book, ***Altars and Foundations.***

As vividly, succinctly, comprehensively and rightly viewed by the author, "An altar is a gateway between the realm of the spirit and the earth realm that grants unhindered access to a spirit being to find legal expressions in the earth. Furthermore, an altar is a legal landing pad of spirits on the earth. The same way we have a landing tarmac for an airplane or a helipad for a helicopter, an altar is the legal landing spot for any kind of spirit, not necessarily demons. Another very important definition of an altar is that it is a token which serves as a seal of a clearly defined covenant between a man and a spirit". This is an area in the Christian faith that a number of believers are too busy to carefully dissect the implications of altars that speak against them. That accounts for why the author submits that, "As powerful and great as God is, if your knowledge of Him has not translated to your knowledge of yourself in Him, then you will probably be walking on the ground like a servant when you should be riding upon horses like royalty" Consequently, the deep knowledge about altars eases victories over battles in the Christian race.

In this well written, appropriately packaged and undoubtedly Holy-Ghost inspired ten chaptered didactic book, the author, himself being a fast rising voice in Biblical teaching ministry, highly gifted with explicating God's word in its most simplistic but effective way, calls the believer's attention to the fact that salvation is just the beginning point of the Christian race. In this book, Pastor Dr Meshach Ileanwa Alfa exposes the implications of altars and more so, the danger in taking altars raised against the believer for granted. Typically simplifying the focus, the author mentions the characteristics of altars as those which include the following; ***The presence of sacrifice, The Desire for Total Influence, The Trans-generational Impact and The influence of altar can only be broken via a legal court process.***

Taking headlong the instances in Canaan, Babylon, Nineveh and Edom and Bible personalities like Moses, David, descendants of king Saul and Abiathar the priest, he challenges the reader to situate these to his own very immediate environment to clearly comprehend why certain things happen the way they do and how you can apply your power of attorney to crush demonic altars raised against you and your destiny.

It is one thing to read, study and meditate upon the Bible. It is yet another thing to have what you read broken down to understandable assimilating levels for faster growth, maturity and conquest as a believer. I have read some works on altars. I am however, yet to come across any work that deals with altars in a situational and personal, risky but conquerable, topical yet universal, simplistic and dynamic, provocative yet inspiring, vivid, revealing and apt like Pastor Dr Meshach Ileanwa Alfa's ***Altars and Foundations.***

I have been so positively battered by my reading of this wonderful gift of a book to the Christian family worldwide. It will be an obvious case of acute selfishness if I delay to very strongly recommend this book to you, all members of your family, friends and church/fellowship members until every child of God accesses, reads and takes action from the reading of this book. Your Christian race can never remain the same after encountering this book.

Once again, congratulations to the author for this unambiguously Holy Ghost-led work.

Rev'd. Prof. Emmy I.U Idegu,
Presiding Labourer,
Odolu Soul Hunt Ministry,
Odolu,
Kogi State,

Contents

INTRODUCTION

"Therefore, if anyone is in Christ, he is a new creation; old things have passed away; behold, all things have become new."

2 Corinthians 5:17

The above scripture describes the dilemma of the believer. While it is true that if anyone is in Christ, he is a new creature, the challenge however is that many times we see certain challenges in our lives that according to our new creation realities shouldn't exist in our lives anymore. We will not be able to come out of this dilemma until we understand that God speaks to us from a prophetic perspective which will always require our understanding of his ways and judicial system to make them realities in our own lives. The Apostle John made this even clearer in his first epistle that although we are already sons of God with all the rights and privileges that should follow, *it doth not yet appear what we shall be* (1 John 3:2 KJV Emphasis mine).

The word of God is always settled and will always stand firm in heaven (Psalm 119:89). In fact, heaven is so stable that there has never been a time where we see God respond to an emergency or a disobedience in heaven, not even the rebellion of Lucifer. The only realm where the word of God is being challenged is in the lives of His people on earth. When Jesus taught His disciples to pray, He specifically taught them to pray that the will of God be done on earth as it is Heaven (Matthew 6:10). This tells us that the will of God is not done on earth automatically, there must always be a judicial system of enforcement which man must understand and engage to make the realities of heaven become our reality here on earth.

The ministry of a *teaching priest* will always be required to help the people comprehend the laws of God that they can engage to access the possibilities of God made available through the finished work of Christ.

For a long time Israel has been without the true God, without a teaching priest, and without law;

2 Chronicles 15:3

The hallmark of a true apostolic ministry therefore must be its ability to bring the people to a place where they fully comprehend the judicial system of God and how they can engage them to appropriate their inheritance based on the finished work of Christ. It is for this purpose that the ministry gifts were given to the Body of Christ.

A true apostolic ministry has the responsibility of not only bringing the Body of Christ into an experience of dimensions of God, but to contribute within the limit of grace towards the building of the Body of Christ in accordance with the requisite proportions and different components so that that edifice can be produced and will fit the description in Revelation 21: 16, a building that is a perfect square with equal length, breadth and height. Since the living stones used for building this edifice are the believers, it therefore makes it necessary to pay attention to the building of the individual believer to experience the possibilities of God in the new creation as we pay attention to the overall edification of the Body of Christ.

I am privileged by grace and election as a *Teaching Priest*, to be privy to some of the revelations of God that have consistently brought me and several others into an experience of the realities of our new life in Christ. Altars and Foundations is one of such teachings that aims to bring balance to the believer's life, authority and walk with God especially in the areas of obtaining justice, deliverance and superimposing the ordinances and speaking of God over pronouncements and generational battles the average believer was born into. We are at war and your victory begins with servicing the right altar as you stand upon a foundation that is sure.

The primary goal of writing this book therefore is to bring us to an understanding of the power of our oneness with Christ and our positional advantage as believers with Him such that we can view the attacks and accusation of Satan through the lens of the finished work of Christ. The book has been segmented into three parts. The first part focuses on the necessity of knowledge as a requisite foundation for enforcing the realities of the new life in Christ Jesus, the second part will take you through a historical perspective of man and altars as a build up to understanding the ordinances that the sacrifice of Jesus has dealt with, while the final part explores the dynamics of the heavenly court, the operation of the accuser of the brethren and the record in heaven, the witness of the Spirit, the Water and the Blood and how they interplay to guarantee our victorious life in Christ Jesus.

I therefore implore you to patiently go through all the pages of this book so you can get the full message that the Lord is bringing your way.

God bless you!

Amen.

PART ONE

KNOWLEDGE

CHAPTER ONE

KNOWLEDGE, THE BEGINNING OF OUR VICTORY

According as his divine power hath given unto us all things that pertain unto life and godliness, through the knowledge of him that hath called us to glory and virtue...

(2 Peter 1:3KJV)

The substitutionary sacrifice of Jesus Christ demonstrated through his death, burial and resurrection completed everything required to give us victory in life. When Jesus said "it is finished" on the cross (John 19:30), it meant that all that was required by divine justice to allow man walk in total and comprehensive victorious life had been satisfied. Like we saw earlier, this is from God's perspective. As far as God is concerned, everyone is already saved and walking in total dominion over the earth and all the works of the devil already. From human experience however, this seems not to be the case. There are still a lot of people going to hell. There are still saved people who are under all manner of oppressions, yet Jesus said, "It is finished". Something must be missing. The scripture that best explains this seeming contrast of prophetic realities versus our experience is Hebrews 2:8-9:

While from the heavenly perspective, all things have already been put under the feet of man meaning he has absolute control over all things, the writer of Hebrews reminds us that from the earth's perspective, we do not yet see all things under man's absolute control but we see Jesus. In other words, Jesus is the evidence that potentially, we have absolute control of all things and as such can walk in total victory and experiential dominion on earth. It is based on this that Peter, the apostle tells us that although His divine power has given us all that pertain to life and godliness, it is only through the knowledge of Him (Jesus Christ) who has called us unto glory and virtue that we can access them experientially. Our labour into the experience of these realities therefore begins in the place of knowledge. These required knowledge are broadly summarized into three:

- Your knowledge of God

- Your knowledge of yourself in God

- Your knowledge of Satan

These are the three dimensional knowledge I believe a Christian should have in order to walk experientially in the victory that Christ already won for us in the kingdom. We shall be looking extensively at these dimensions of knowledge in the next three chapters.

CHAPTER TWO

YOUR KNOWLEDGE OF GOD

The knowledge of God is infinite but there are specific attributes of God that we must know that will guide us in our approach to Him for our inheritance. We need to understand the multi - faceted dimension of His operations and the different possibilities that those dimensions can produce in our lives on earth. The dealings of God with man in the Old Testament is entirely different from his dealings with man in the New Testament. So we shall be exploring the various dimensions of the dealings of God under both.

We admit that man is limited in his ability to peer into the infinite to understand the boundless possibilities and infinite dimensions of God. We cannot talk exhaustively in this section about the multi-faceted dimensions of God in His glory. Nevertheless, I would focus on four dimensions of God with respect to His dealings with man.

1. *The Dimension of God as a Father*

In this manner, therefore, pray: Our Father...

(Matt 6:9)

The first dimension of God we must know on our journey to enforcing our victory and dominion is the dimension of God as our Father. This dimension which is the most important was not known by the people under the Old Testament. It was the birth of our Lord Jesus Christ that revealed this dimension of God as a Father.

Behold what manner of love the Father has bestowed on us, that we should be called children of God!...

1 John 3:1

The dimension of God as our Father means that we have been brought into a relationship with Him through faith in His Son Jesus Christ. This relationship grants us the right of inheritance to all that He has. Jesus will say that all that the Father has are His (John 16:15). God as our Father loves us and is willing to give us whatever we ask of Him (John 16:23, 27). The dimension of God as our Father requires no intermediary, not even Jesus (John 16:26) because we have direct access to Him by reason of our relationship with Him. God as our Father will always give what is good to His children (Matt. 7:11) because it has always been the Father's good pleasure to give us the kingdom (Luke 12:32)

It is the dimension of God as Father that is responsible for all the prophetic realities we are talking about. If all there is to God is His dimension as a Father, then every believer should be walking experientially in total victory and absolute dominion over creation. Sadly, there is more to God than being a Father. His dimension as a Father is exclusively known and experienced by those who have acknowledged Jesus as their Lord and saviour.

If God is not yet your Father, then repeat this prayer by faith:

Lord Jesus, I believe with my heart that you are the Son of God, that you took my place in death and you rose again from the dead to give me life, you became sin that I may become the righteousness of God, I confess with my mouth that you are my Lord and my Saviour, by faith in you, I receive eternal life into my spirit. Thank God I'm born again. In Jesus name I've prayed, Amen.

Congratulations! You are now born again and have become a child of God. Feel very free to call God "Father."

2. The Dimension of God as King

---

*For the Lord is our Judge, the Lord is our Lawgiver, the **Lord is our King**; He will save us...*

Isaiah 33:22 *(Emphasis mine)*

The second dimension of God that the believer must encounter to walk experientially and activate divine realities in Christ is the dimension of God as King. God as King reveals His absolute dominion over the entire universe. He is in

Charge. In Him all things consist. The King does not need the opinion of anyone to declare his counsel. Kings make decrees. The word of a king is law. The Psalmist describes the King dimension of God as follows:

For the Lord is the great God, and the great King above all gods

(Psalms 95:3)

Solomon in buttressing this also said:

Where the word of a king is, there is power; and who may say to him, "What are you doing?

(Ecclesiastes 8:4)

The Lord God is our King. His dominion is everlasting, of the increase of His Government and peace, there is no end. He is the *King of kings and the Lord of lords* (Revelation 19:6). Even Nebuchadnezzar in the peak of his pride acknowledged Him as the God of gods and Lord of kings (Daniel 2:47). You must know that our God is not a president, who was voted into power and has a tenure that can elapse. He is not the first among many gods, He is the only God. His throne is not threatened. From everlasting to Everlasting, He remains the owner and controller of the universe. Every time a man saw

God from Genesis to Revelation, he saw God seated. Kings sit only when there is rest so there has never been a situation that warranted God being in an emergency standing mode. He is not scratching His head wondering what to do with earth. He is the King. He has everything absolutely under control. This should give you peace.

The only time we saw God stand was when Jesus stood to receive Stephen. It was not because there was an emergency that needed something to be done quickly to produce results. Just imagine how unlimited, unstoppable and invincible you will be when your Father is the King. Hallelujah!

3. The Dimension of God as Lawgiver

---

*For the Lord is our Judge, the **Lord is our Lawgiver**, the Lord is our King; He will save us...*

Isaiah 33:22 *(Emphasis mine)*

The third dimension of God the believer needs to know to walk experientially in the realities of the new life in Christ is the dimension of God as the Lawgiver.

When Joshua was going to step into the shoes of Moses as the leader of Israel in their journey from the land of bandage to the land of promise, Joshua was understandably afraid looking at the enormity of the task ahead of him. Joshua witness Moses' contest with magicians in Egypt, watched him path the red sea in the presence of an angry crowd and witnessed many times the rebellion of the people against Moses and even God. He was obviously wondering how he would lead this people to the land of promise, then God gave him an instruction that would guarantee his success in that endeavour. Let's look at that instruction very quickly:

*This Book of the **Law** shall not depart from your mouth, but you shall meditate in it day and night, that you may observe to do according to all that is written in it. For then you will make your way prosperous, and then you will have good success.*

Joshua 1:8 *(Emphasis mine)*

What God was simply telling Joshua is that Moses did not succeed just because he was Moses. He succeeded because of his access to the Laws of God. God packaged His secret codes of operation into Laws and handed them over to us to make our outcomes predictable. So, anyone who engages the Book of the Laws of God in the three dimensions described in the scripture above is guaranteed to make his way prosperous and have good success.

In the peak of Job's predicament, God asked him a very interesting question.

Do you know the laws of the heavens? Can you set up [God's] dominion over the earth (Job 38:33 NIV)? In other words, Job! You will be able to replicate the dominion of God over the earth only if you know the laws of the heavens. The activation of your victory as a child of God therefore, begins with your encounter with the Lawgiver because *the law of the Lord is perfect, converting the soul... (Psalms 19:7).*

Even though the Psalmist was referring to the Mosaic Law in this scripture, the Mosaic Law is no longer applicable to us in the New Testament because *Christ is the end of the law for righteousness to everyone who believes* (Romans 10:4). This doesn't mean that God is no longer the Lawgiver. What has changed is the law. He has given us a new law which is love.

30'...And you shall love the Lord your God with all your heart, with all your soul, with all your mind, and with all your strength.' This is the first commandment. 31And the second, like it, is this: 'You shall love your neighbour as yourself.' There is no other commandment greater than these.

Mark 12:30-31

34A new commandment I give to you, that you love one another; as I have loved you, that you also love one another. 35By this all will know that you are My disciples, if you have love for one another."

John 13:34-35

¹²This is My commandment, that you love one another as I have loved you... ¹⁷These things I command you, that you love one another.

John 15:12,17

*⁸Owe no one anything except to love one another, **for he who loves another has fulfilled the law.** ⁹For the commandments, "You shall not commit adultery," "You shall not murder," "You shall not steal," "You shall not bear false witness," "You shall not covet," and if there is any other commandment, are all summed up in this saying, namely, "You shall love your neighbour as yourself." ¹⁰Love does no harm to a neighbour; therefore **love is the fulfilment of the law.***

Rom 13:8-10 *(Emphasis mine)*

The Lord is our Lawgiver and the new law is LOVE, first for God and then for one another!

4. The Dimension of God as Judge

The fourth and final dimension of God that the believer must encounter to walk in the realities of the new life in Christ is the dimension of God as Judge. The revelation of God as Judge in the Old Testament is entirely different from that of the New. If the Law has changed, then the understanding of the Judge should also change. We shall first look at the dimension of God as Judge in the Old Testament so we can build a good foundation to understanding this dimension in the New Testament.

God as Judge in the Old Testament

It was the patriarch, Abraham that called God "the Judge of all the earth" who is expected to do right (Genesis 18:25). He said this with respect to God's ability to distinguish the guilty from the innocent and the wicked from the righteous. God was going to destroy Sodom and Gomorrah where Abraham's nephew lived at the time. This was because of the level of wickedness, evil and depravity in the land. God gave the information to Abraham His friend but Abraham approached God from a judicial dimension to plead for the exemption of

Lot. This dimension of God is the core of this book you are holding in your hand.

A judge is someone who is authorized to decide cases in the law court. A judge is neutral and impartial, guided only by the law and not by emotions or sentiments. He is required by the scale of justice to give equal opportunity to both the prosecutor and the accused to present their respective defence. He measures the strength of both sides based on the law and then presents his judgement.

A judge does not veto a case; he decides a case by looking at the respective arguments through the lens of the written law. Your ability to present your case, defend it and quote relevant laws and precedence that support your argument is a determinant factor when appealing to the Lord who is judge. He then looks at it and based on the evidence available to Him, gives you justice or otherwise.

I often wonder why God didn't veto the matter of Job but granted Satan's request twice to deal with Job. Something was lacking in the life of Job. Elihu speaking by the Spirit showed us what was lacking.

19"Man is also chastened with pain on his bed, And with strong pain in many of his bones, 20So that his life abhors bread, And his soul succulent food. 21His flesh wastes away from sight, And his bones stick out which once were not seen. 22Yes, his soul draws near the Pit, And his life to the executioners. 23"If there is a messenger for him, A mediator, one among a

thousand, To show man His uprightness,
24Then He is gracious to him, and says,
'Deliver him from going down to the Pit; I
have found a ransom'; *25His flesh shall be*
young like a child's, He shall return to the days
of his youth. 26He shall pray to God, and He will
delight in him, He shall see His face with joy,
For He restores to man His righteousness.

Job 33:19-26 *(Emphasis mine)*

What was lacking in the case of Job is a Ransom. Jesus Christ is our Ransom. Our case cannot be like that of Job anymore. We will then explore the dimension of God as Judge in the New Testament.

God as Judge in the New Testament

Is God still our Judge in the New Testament? Will God still Judge us His Children in the New Testament as He did in the Old? We will answer these questions by asking another question. If the law has changed in the New Testament, will the system of Judgement remain the same? Let's look at the words of Jesus Himself.

22For the Father judges no one, but has committed all judgment to the Son… 27and has given Him authority to execute judgment also, because He is the Son of Man.

John 5:22, 27

God has entrusted all judgements in the New Testament to His Son Jesus Christ. Jesus Himself tells us the nature of that judgement as the Holy Spirit would reveal.

8And when He has come, He will convict the world of sin, and of righteousness, and of judgment: 9of sin, because they do not believe in Me; 10of righteousness, because I go to My Father and you see Me no more; 11of judgment, because the ruler of this world is judged.

John 16:8-11

Isn't it interesting that one of the primary responsibilities of the Holy Spirit is to bring us the conviction that the prince of this world, our adversary has been condemned already? What accusation can a condemned entity called Satan bring against the elect that shall stand? None.

The single reason why believers go through all manner of satanic oppressions as though Jesus Christ died in vain is that they have not understood the difference between the justice system of God in the Old and the New Testaments. Satan explores their ignorance of the significance of the finished work of Christ in their lives and their relationship. They are in lack of what has been freely given to them by God.

5But also for this very reason, giving all diligence, add to your faith virtue, to virtue

*knowledge, ⁶to knowledge self-control, to
self-control perseverance, to perseverance
godliness, ⁷to godliness brotherly kindness,
and to brotherly kindness love. ⁸For if these
things are yours and abound, you will be
neither barren nor unfruitful in the
knowledge of our Lord Jesus Christ.* **⁹For he
who lacks these things is short-sighted,
even to blindness, and has forgotten that
he was cleansed from his old sins***.*

2 Peter 1:5-9 *(Emphasis mine)*

My understanding of the interplay of these dimensions of God has drastically changed my approach to God in prayers.

A Classic Illustration of the Multifaceted Dimension of God

Many years ago, God used a strange way to teach me the importance of understanding these four dimensions of His operations with respect to divine justice. I saw a home video, Silent Night and in the movie, a man who was a judge had a son that was involved in an armed robbery. The son was then arrested and brought before his father as a judge. The wife; the boy's mother begged the judge, her husband to save their son but the father's hands were tied. The overwhelming evidence before him that pointed to the fact that his son was a criminal and deserved to die far outweighed his saving power as a father. The heart of the father wanted to save him, the office of the judge prevented him and a father sentenced his own son to death by the firing squad.

The difference however is that Jesus Christ has already gone to the cross for the same sin for which we are being accused. It is unlawful for a man to be punished twice for the same offence. When Jesus went to that cross, we went with Him. Our Father who is the Judge has already sentenced us to death which happened when we were crucified with Christ at Calvary (Galatians 2:20).

I have been crucified with Christ; it is no longer I who live, but Christ lives in me; and the life which I now live in the flesh I live by faith in the Son of God, who loved me and gave Himself for me.

Galatians 2:20

We are not just vindicated because of the Father's Love for us, we are vindicated because full justice have been served. The sin for which Satan brings accusations against us has been fully punished at Calvary. We are no longer guilty! We are New Creations in Christ Jesus. Hallelujah!

CHAPTER THREE

YOUR KNOWLEDGE OF YOURSELF IN GOD

Second to your knowledge of God in His multifaceted dimensions is your knowledge of yourself in God. As powerful and great as God is, if your knowledge of Him has not translated to your knowledge of yourself in Him, then you will probably be walking on the ground like a servant when you should be riding upon horses like royalty. Hear the words of King Solomon:

> *I have seen servants on horses, while princes walk on the ground like servants.*
>
> **Ecclesiastes 10:7**

The Psalmist also emphasised this in the following scripture:

> *A man who is in honour, yet does not understand, is like the beasts that perish.*
>
> **Psalms 49:20**

Our relationship with the Father through the finished work of Christ has brought us to a realm of unimaginable honour –

we are sons of the most high. We can perish as mere men this notwithstanding if we do not pay the price to know the implication of our new life in Christ.

**⁵They do not know, nor do they understand; *they walk about in darkness; all the foundations of the earth are unstable.* *⁶I said, "You are gods, and all of you are children of the Most High.* ⁷But you shall die like men, *and fall like one of the princes."*

Psalms 82:5-7 *(Emphasis mine)*

The tragedy is simply in the ignorance. There is a way a child of God shouldn't die. There are things that shouldn't happen to you by reason of your new life in Christ. We have the greatest honour of being called the children of God. We must press on to know the implication of that so that we can walk in its realities.

Let's take a look at a very interesting scripture that clearly explains what we are talking about:

---

¹³When Jesus came into the region of Caesarea Philippi, He asked His disciples, saying, "Who do men say that I, the Son of Man, am?" ¹⁴So they said," Some say John the Baptist, some Elijah, and others Jeremiah or one of the prophets." ¹⁵He said to them, "But who do you say that I am?" ¹⁶Simon Peter *answered and said, **"You are the Christ, the Son of the living God."**[17]Jesus answered and said to him, "Blessed are you, Simon Bar-Jonah, for flesh and blood has not revealed this to you, but My Father who is in heaven. [18]**And I also say to you that you are Peter,** and on this rock I will build My church, and the gates of Hades shall not prevail against it. [19]And I will give you the keys of the kingdom of heaven, and whatever you bind on earth will be bound in heaven, and whatever you loose on earth will be loosed in heaven."*

***Matthew 16:13-19** (Emphasis mine)*

Jesus was at the verge of concluding His earthly ministry and handover to the disciples He had been training for about three years. After sampling their opinion on what people think about His personality, He asked them this question to test their revelation of His personality and power. **"Who do you say that I am?" (vs.15)**. In other words, "you have told me what others have to say about me, but it's important I know what you that I have been training for about three years have to say about me". Peter, finally settling on an answer by the spirit said, **"You are the Christ, the son of the living God" (vs.16)**. Jesus goes on to reveal a powerful key in His answer: "Flesh and blood has not revealed this to you but my Father who is in heaven" (vs. 17).

It is not given to a man to know what and who God is by human calculation or logic. You can only know who and what

God is to the degree that He chooses to reveal Himself to you. The end of that revelation however, is that who you are in your knowledge of who He is must be revealed to you. You will only confront darkness on the strength of your knowledge of who you are in who He is. For instance, He told Moses that He has made him God unto Pharaoh (Exodus 7:1). With what consciousness do you think Moses will approach Pharaoh? He will approach him as though God was there in person.

There is a dimension of yourself you will never know until the dimension of God responsible for revealing that dimension of yourself is revealed to you. So Jesus told Peter, since I have been revealed to you as Christ, the Son of the living God, I also reveal to you that you are not just Simon (reed that is weak and frail and can easily be broken) but Peter, a solid rock upon which I can confidently build my Church that is invincible to the gates of hell (Vs.17-18). This means that people can confidently confront the gates of hell not just because they know that God is powerful but they stem from the all-powerful God like rocks.

In a nutshell, Jesus was simply saying, "I cannot build a church based on your knowledge of me alone. Your knowledge of me should produce something that will be a foundation upon which I can build something. "Your life is built on what you have discovered as your place in Christ. You need to understand the power of our oneness with Him and have an even more powerful understanding of our positional advantage as believers with Him. Your knowledge of God must translate to your **knowledge of yourself in God!**

CHAPTER FOUR

YOUR KNOWLEDGE OF SATAN

*Be sober, be vigilant; because your
adversary the devil walks about like a
roaring lion, seeking whom he may devour.*

1 Peter 5:8

There is a third dimension of knowledge which a believer should have in order to walk in the reality of our victory in Christ Jesus. After knowing God in His multifaceted dimensions, knowing yourself in God, there are basic things you ought to know about Satan. I am not trying to postulate a theory that advocates for an extensive study of Satan. In fact, there are several details about Satan that are totally unnecessary for us to know as believers. However, there are certain information we must have about him in line with the truth of scripture that are necessary for our experiential dominion. I will discuss them under two broad categories.

1. *The Implication of the Finished Work of Christ on Satan.*

Think with me for a moment, when Satan hears the blood of Jesus, what comes to his mind? What does he think when you mention the name of Jesus? What effect does it have on him? Ask yourself, "What is Satan's current position relative to me?" Where is Satan relative to me? If I am addressing Satan should I look up or down? Where is he? There are certain things you must know about Satan to remain victorious.

The death, burial and resurrection of our Lord and Saviour Jesus Christ did not only have implications on us. It has an implication on Satan as well. What exactly is this implication? It is captured in the following scripture:

In this way God took away Satan's power to accuse you of sin, and God openly displayed to the whole world Christ's triumph at the cross where your sins were all taken away."

Colossians 2:15 (TLB)

Another translation puts it this way:

He stripped all the spiritual tyrants in the universe of their sham authority at the Cross and marched them naked through the streets.

Colossians 2:15 (THE MESSAGE)

Satan has been eternally stripped of his power to accuse you of any sin. This knowledge is very fundamental to our walking in victory. All the punishment for your sin has been fully served. Jesus paid it all. Satan has no ground to bring accusation against you anymore. The question you may want to ask is this; if Satan has been stripped of his power to accuse us, how then does he still operate to stop the blessing of the believer?

2. The Strategies of Satan

The second thing you need to know about Satan is his strategies. Jesus told us that all powers in heaven, on earth, beneath the earth have been given to Him… (Matthew 28:18-20).This notwithstanding, we still see Satan wielding some level of power over believers as it were bringing all manner of afflictions and oppression upon them. We still see Satan bringing accusations against God's precious people day and night. What power is he using exactly? It noteworthy that, the legal grip that Satan had over this earth was broken and Satan was cast out as recorded (John 12:31).

I realized that Satan is not necessarily so powerful. The power Satan uses against believers is deceit. The strength of Satan is his ability to hide in darkness. If his strategies are known, they become powerless.

------

*Put on the whole armour of God that you may be able to **stand against the wiles of the devil**.*

***Ephesians 6:11-12** (Emphasis mine)*

The Bible never instructed us to put on the whole armour of God to fight against the powers of Satan. He said to fight against the wiles of the devil (Schemes in the NIV; Strategies and tricks in TLB). Satan's greatest advantage is not power, it is a tool so subtle many believers have fallen for it, never to recover.

Paul, the apostle speaking in 2 Corinthians 2:11 said:

Lest Satan should get an advantage of us: for we are not ignorant of his devices.

2 Corinthians 2:11 (KJV)

The word 'get' is quite disturbing. The Bible didn't say lest he takes advantage of us, he said lest he gets. This means if Satan succeeds in making you ignorant of his strategies, the advantage is in his hands already. It's not that he's trying to get it. The only thing that Satan needs to do for the advantage over your life as a Christian to be in his hand is that he deceives you to be ignorant of his devices. The Living Bible puts it in a very interesting way:

*A further reason for forgiveness is **to keep from being outsmarted by Satan,** for we know what he is trying to do.*

2 Corinthians 2:11 *(TLB Emphasis mine)*

Satan is not so powerful. The ability of Satan to deceive or outsmart you is his greatest advantage!

A believer who does not understand how Satan operates will be cheated and defeated by Satan. The nature of his operation is such that where he actually touches or disturbs in your life might not necessarily be where his interest lies. Satan first distracts you before he launches his major attack on you. The least of the saints can stop Satan, however, his ability to shield himself in darkness becomes the advantage he has over believers and Paul tells us that all things are made manifest by the light (Ephesians 5:13).

Can we have a closer look at Ephesians 6: 11 once again. Paul admonishes believers to "Put in the whole armour of God that ye may be able to stand against the wiles of the devil." The word 'wiles' there means deceit, hidden strategies, tricks and schemes of the devil.

In the next verse, Paul continues, "For we wrestle not against flesh and blood but against principalities, against powers, against rulers of darkness of this world, against spiritual wickedness in high places..." The Living Bible's translation says,

---

*For we are not fighting against people made
of flesh and blood but against persons
without bodies, the evil rulers of the unseen
world, those mighty satanic beings, great
evil princes of darkness who rule this world
and against huge numbers of different
spirits in the spirit world.*

Our enemies are persons without bodies. If we must be able to stand and utterly enforce our victory over them, we must sustain spiritual intelligence enough to first uncover their strategies and then stand vehemently against them until all that Christ paid for becomes our experience here and now.

Let me reiterate a few truths I shared in my book, "Spiritual Dominion" about Satan.

- Satan is NOT the opposite of God! He was created by God and there was a time he did not exist. God did not create him as Satan, his choice for rebellion changed him from Lucifer (light bearer) to Satan (accuser).

- God and Satan are not in a battle. NO! The battle for dominion is between MAN and SATAN not God and Satan. The battle only concerns God because man was created in God's image and likeness.

- Satan does not enslave believers with power, he enslaves them through deception.

- Satan has powers but he is not omnipotent (All powerful). There is a limit to his power and he knows that.

- Satan is not omniscient. He doesn't know everything. In fact, the things he knows about us are minute compared to the ones he doesn't know.

- Satan is not omnipresent. In other words, he lacks the ability to be everywhere at the same time.

PART TWO
MAN AND ALTARS

CHAPTER FIVE

MAN: A UNIQUE CREATION

26Then God said, "Let Us make man in Our image, according to Our likeness; let them have dominion over the fish of the sea, over the birds of the air, and over the cattle, over all the earth and over every creeping thing that creeps on the earth." 27So God created man in His own image; in the image of God He created him; male and female He created them. 28Then God blessed them, and God said to them, "Be fruitful and multiply; fill the earth and subdue it; have dominion over the fish of the sea, over the birds of the air, and over every living thing that moves on the earth.

Genesis 1:26-28

The creation of man was very unique. In verse 26, God stated clearly that the reason He wanted to create man was that the man should have dominion over all that He had created. In other words God was creating an administrator, one who will rule and govern His creation. The jurisdiction of man's assignment (the earth) necessitated his unique design as we will see shortly.

In Genesis 1:27, God created man in His own image... What exactly is the image of God? Jesus tells us in John 4:24 that God is a Spirit. Comparing this with Genesis 1:27, we can say that God created man a spirit. Since God is a Spirit, the man He created in His image in Genesis 1:27 must be a spirit as well. However, the spirit-man cannot adapt to the earth which is his sphere of dominion without possessing a body formed from the materials of the earth. I call this spiritual adaptation. This was demonstrated by the following three New Testament accounts.

1. The legion's request to be cast into the swine

---

*⁹Then He asked him, "What is your name?" And he answered, saying, "My name is Legion; for we are many." ¹⁰Also he begged Him earnestly that He would not send them out of the country. ¹¹Now a large herd of swine was feeding there near the mountains. ¹²**So all the demons begged Him, saying, "Send us to the swine, that we may enter them."** ¹³And at once Jesus gave them permission. Then the unclean spirits went out and entered the swine (there were about two thousand); and the herd ran violently down the steep place into the sea, and drowned in the sea.*

***Mark 5:9-13** (Emphasis mine)*

The reason the demons asked Jesus' permission to go into the swine was that they wanted to have bodies that would grant them legitimate access to that territory since Jesus had asked them to come out of the man. They still lost that legitimacy because the herd of swine drowned in the river.

2. The evil spirit that couldn't find rest for his soul

---

43 "When an unclean spirit goes out of a man, he goes through dry places, seeking rest, and finds none. 44Then he says, 'I will return to my house from which I came'...

Matthew 12:43-44

This is another classical demonstration of the illegitimacy of a spirit's operation on earth without a body. As long as the unclean spirit was inside a body, it had rest but the moment it exited that body it began to seek rest in other bodies and not finding any decided to return to its former house.

3. The immaculate conception of Jesus Christ.

...Behold, the young woman who is unmarried and a virgin shall conceive and

bear a son, and shall call his name
Immanuel [God with us].

Isaiah 7:14 (AMP)

And the angel answered and said to her,
*"**The Holy Spirit will come upon you**, and*
the power of the Highest will overshadow
you; therefore, also, that Holy One who is to
*be born will be called **the Son of God**.*

Luke 1:35 *(Emphasis mine)*

The third and most important demonstration of this law of territory was the Immaculate Conception and birth of our Lord Jesus Christ. The name of the Child as prophesied by Isaiah the Prophet was a demonstration of the intent of God which we saw fulfilled in Revelation 21:3. God who is a Spirit wanted to come to the earth and operate legitimately to bring salvation to man. He had to request for the permission of the Virgin Mary to partner with Him by allowing her womb provide the body that would house Him and give Him legitimacy in what He had come to do. Even the Holy Spirit when he came to make His abode on earth had to indwell men.

Man's Unique Design continues...

As a result of this law of territory, man the Spirit created in Genesis 1:27 needed to be provided with a body formed from the materials of the earth in order to carry out his dominion task in the earth. The second account of man's creation we see in Chapter 2 of Genesis is that of the body of man.

And the Lord God formed man of the dust of the ground...

Genesis 2:7a

Man as the image of God could not adapt to the regions of the earth without being made from the materials of the earth where he is supposed to rule. So God made a body for the man. The body is not the man. He made a body for the man, the same thing He did for Jesus.

*⁵Therefore, when He came into the world, He said: "Sacrifice and offering You did not desire, **But a body You have prepared for Me.** ⁶In burnt offerings and sacrifices for sin You had no pleasure. ⁷Then I said, 'Behold, I have come — In the volume of the book it is written of Me — **To do Your will, O God.**'"*

Hebrews 10:5-7 *(Emphasis mine)*

The will mentioned in the scripture above is to be done on earth and that is why the Spirit must have a body.

Apart from the Spirit-man created in the very image of God and the body formed from the dust of the earth to house that Spirit, there was a third component God introduced into this unique creation.

...and [God] breathed into his nostrils the breath of life; and man became a living soul.

Genesis 2:7b *(KJV Emphasis mine)*

The spirit and the body of man function from different realms, thus will have very serious difficulty in comprehending one another. Paul, the apostle explained this dilemma in 1 Corinthians 2:

But the natural man does not receive the things of the Spirit of God...

1 Corinthians 2:14

The Spirit-man was created in the very image of God, thus does not have a problem communing with the Spirit of God and the realm of the spirit. This man was unlimited. The body however was created from the earth, thus can only understand the language of the earth. It is absolutely impossible for these two entities to communicate. What language will they speak - that of heaven or the earth? It is for this reason that God introduced an intermediary or interface between the Spirit man and his body. This interface has the ability to comprehend the language of the Spirit realm and also communicate to the body in the language of the earth. This interface is an interpreter that has the capability of speaking the language of both realms. This interface is called the mind. It has an intellect with the ability to reason and interpret the impulses of the spirit based on a pre-programmed information database, it has the emotion which is the communicator of the conclusions of the intellect and a will which is the force behind the execution of what has been concluded. This is what we popularly refer to as the soul. Simply put, God gave man a soul compartment to interface between the Spirit and the body. Man became a living soul. The soul given to man became the intermediary that interprets the impulses of the spirit for the body to execute because dominion has to be communicated in a language understood by the earth. Man became the only creature that has this unique configuration. He became the only entity with legitimate jurisdiction of operation covering both the realm of the spirit and the realm of the earth. This means that he can be in the realm of the earth and the realm of the spirit at the same time. It's so serious that God had to become man in order to function in this capacity.

To test this unique design of man, God brought all the animals to man to see what he would name them and the Bible says whatsoever name Adam called it - it didn't say that became its name - it said that was the name. That means the animals were named before they were brought to Adam but the information about the names were not revealed to Adam. Adam without consulting God named them. So Adam didn't have to say, "God what should I call this?" It was Adam's decision to call a lion, lion and God said" I named it lion before I brought it to you." His spirit picked the impulses from God and his mind interpreted what was received correctly.

This was the level of intelligence that man operated with until tragedy struck. Man fell and was reduced to guesswork. The Bible says that they made aprons of fig leaves and covered themselves (Genesis 3:7). When God came, He made them a coat of animal skin (Genesis 3:21). Imagine the difference in sophistication, fig leaf versus animal skin, apron versus coat. Man suddenly lost that intelligence because the God nature in him that made him reason like God had left. He lost that image, that spiritual system that made him function like God. Man died spiritually. He fell short of the glory of God (Romans 3:23).

So from that time there was a desire in the heart of the mortal man to access the realm of the spirit because there resided a possibility beyond his human existence. From that time, man embarked on a search and began to intercourse with all manner of wisdom, spirits and began to enter into certain covenants with them so that they can grant him access to the realm of the spirit he was interfacing naturally. This was the origin of altars as we will see in the next chapter.

CHAPTER SIX

ALTARS: A SPIRITUAL PARTNERSHIP

What is an Altar?

An altar is a gateway between the realm of the spirit and the earth realm that grants unhindered access to a spirit being to find legal expressions in the earth. Furthermore, an altar is a legal landing pad of spirits on the earth. The same way we have a landing tarmac for an airplane or a helipad for a helicopter, an altar is the legal landing spot for any kind of spirit, not necessarily demons. Another very important definition of an altar is that it is a token which serves as a seal of a clearly defined covenant between a man and a spirit.

Over time, we see that families and territories have activated altars, some unto God and several others, unto some spirits that gave them momentary results for a while and suddenly began to take things from them.

Origin of Altars

As we saw in the previous chapter, the fullness of man's dominion on earth was dependent on his ability to interact effectively with both the realm of the spirit and the realm of the earth. The Garden of Eden itself was a place of interaction between God and man (Genesis 3:8). As a consequence of the fall, he was banished from the garden, thus lost access to the River that flowed from Eden – the Holy Spirit (Genesis 2:10; cf. John 7:37-39). He lost his access to the Fountain of unlimited wisdom and power, the very Breath of the Almighty God. He lost the very communion and intimacy with the Holy Spirit which was responsible for his unlimited access to the realm of the spirit.

On the other hand, the earth had always been the centre of attraction to all spirits. Since they cannot access the earth legitimately without the authorization of man in whose authority the earth had been entrusted, and man himself was now limited because of his fall, there was a partnership between man and these spirits so that man could give them authorization to come to the earth. What was the nature of this partnership? The spirits, in exchange for authorized access promised to grant man access to the possibilities beyond the capabilities of man. Every spirit, including the Holy Spirit required this partnership to exert influence upon the earth. This authorization was made by what we now call **altars**.

Interestingly, it is not only the Holy Spirit that can grant a man access to the possibilities in the realm of the spirit. All spirits can grant man access to possibilities in the realm of the spirit, the only difference is the kind of possibility. This is why some people worship ancestors and different kinds of animals. The Holy Spirit, however is the only Spirit authorized by God to grant man access to the realm of the spirit to bring forth possibilities that will be to the glory of God.

To access the possibilities of the realm of the spirit through the Holy Spirit, a man must die first. However, men not willing to go through this painful and yet necessary process took the shorter route through other spirits.

When God chased Adam out of the garden, the Bible says that He placed at the entrance of the garden, Cherubim and a flaming sword (Gen. 3:24). I used to think that he placed cherubim carrying a flaming sword. He placed Cherubim and a flaming sword. The Psalmist tells us that where the cherubim's are, there the throne of God is (Psalms 99:1 KJV). When Moses was instructed to build the Ark of the Covenant, God asked Him to build a Mercy Seat of pure gold upon which should be placed two cherubim. God told Moses that He would commune with him from a point above the mercy seat and between the cherubim. The mercy seat and the cherubim were a similitude of the pattern of the throne of God that Moses saw on the mount (Exodus 25:17-22). So the presence of the Cherubim at the entrance of the garden means that God took His throne and placed it at the entrance of the garden.

It was not just the throne He placed there, the Bible tells us that the word of God is sharper than a two - edged sword piercing unto the dividing asunder of soul and spirit (Heb. 4:12). The TREE OF LIFE is equally typical of the CROSS or Christ Himself, who gives life more abundantly. This means the flaming sword is Word of God Himself, such that nobody can access the tree of life without first encountering the sword and when you meet the sword, the sword must divide and discern the thought and the intents of the hearts of men. This means that no man can ever access the Tree of Life again without first passing through the flaming sword which will not only cut but will burn whatever represents chaff. Men not willing to go through this process began to boycott and look for other spirits that could grant them access to certain possibilities inherent in the realm of the spirit.

This was the origin of witchcraft. We then saw in Genesis 6 how the fallen angels beheld the daughters of the sons of men as fair and began to take them for wives. They began to intercourse with the daughters of men and the Bible says that sons were born unto these fallen spirits. What kind of offspring would you expect to come from this kind of union? You guessed right. They began to give birth to hybrid humans. They gave birth to giants through whom the fallen spirits became legal inhabitants of the earth and multiplied evil so much that Noah was the only blameless man living on earth at that time (Genesis 6:9 NLT).This began the activation of certain forms of witchcraft and divinations upon the face of the earth and evil began to increase so much that the Bible testified that Noah was a just and perfect man in his generation.

Characteristics of Altars

There are certain characteristics that define an altar. We will look at a few of them.

1. **The presence of sacrifice:**

An altar is an altar because it is used for sacrifice. Remember, the realm of the Spirit wants to interact with the earth realm legally right? And the earth wants to interact with the realm of the spirit because the inhabitants of the earth know that without the realm of the spirit, they are limited in the results they can produce. So they call for the assistance of these spirit beings. In agreement to bring these possibilities to the inhabitants of the earth, the spirits give conditions - certain things that can be done to create a habitation that will look exactly like where they are coming from. And then they summarize their demands in what they call a sacrifice and ask men to raise certain structures to put certain sacrifices.

The kind of sacrifices upon the altar is dependent on the kind of spirit that wants to access the earth through that altar. The absence of sacrifice upon an altar makes it unqualified to be called an altar. Without sacrifice, an altar is but a stone or anything that was raised. A sacrifice is what makes it an altar. The kind of spirit to whom the altar is raised determines whether the altar will be a good or bad one. So if it is raised to God -remember that the Bible says we should present our bodies as living sacrifices- this means that the minimum requirement to make the Holy Spirit come to the earth to assist you is that your body - not an animal, not your money becomes a living sacrifice offered to Him. In the same way, demon spirits have their demands as to the things that qualify to bring them to the earth. For instance, there are demonic spirits that require the sacrifice of incest, extramarital sexual relationship, and homosexuality, amongst others. The character of the spirit is reflected in the kind of sacrifice they demand for.

Some of the sacrifices are not necessarily animals. They can just be certain abstinence from some things. I remember some years ago when I was in secondary school, we had a cook who for thirty days didn't have her bath. Imagine a woman who abstained from water for thirty days! She was cooking for us and we were eating. We discovered a foul odour was coming from her and not from the food and we decided to ask. She said that their deity said she was not to have her bath for a period of time. That was a sacrifice. She is not an animal but if she was able to do that completely then there was a possibility such an experience itself was to activate.

The prophets of baal were cutting themselves as a sacrifice to bring baal to Mount Carmel (1 Kings 18:28). Similarly, when you pray in a particular place consistently for a long time, the sacrifice of prayer in that place turns that place into a prayer altar. Typical examples are the Lawn Tennis Court at the Ahmadu Bello University, Zaria where I schooled and a place like the Moravian falls in South Carolina, USA.

2. The Desire for Total Influence

One of the things that make the subject of altars quite serious is that the demands are not only binding on the individual who activated it but on everything connected to that individual. Every partnership has terms and conditions, benefits and obligations. Every spirit, including the Holy Spirit expects the total allegiance of man in exchange for partnership. For the Holy Spirit, what He gets in return is your whole being. For every one of these spirits, their allegiance to you is primarily because of the territories on earth that is within your jurisdiction that you will bring under their control. A business of a business man who has activated an altar comes under the influence of that altar.

3. The Trans-generational Impact

Altars often outlive the person who established them. Their validity is trans-generational. Perhaps you are thinking, "I am a young single brother that is trying to make ends meet who invoked a spirit and entered into a covenant. I thought I did it alone..." The spirit sees your children, your children's children and four or five generations from you. He knows that it is not just you and if he can get you to sign an agreement with him, he knows there are other people he can get. So many people are under influences of covenants that were entered generations before they were born. They find themselves as Christians but are being driven by possibilities they can't explain because certain things were activated on their behalf that ignorance of the justice system of God has kept active. This ought not to be so because it is clear from scriptures that we have been translated from the poor of darkness into the kingdom of God's dear son (Colossian). This is why this book is written, to bring us to the point of understanding the significance of the finished work of Christ in our lives so that Satan does take advantage of our ignorance anymore.

Look at the life of Abraham for example. When he got to the land of Canaan after God had told him to leave his father's house, the Bible tells us that he raised an altar unto God between Bethel and Hai (or Ai), where he had pitched his tent

---

⁷Then the Lord appeared to Abram and said,
"To your descendants I will give this land."
And there he built an altar to the Lord,
who had appeared to him. *⁸And he moved*

We can see account of Abraham building his first altar. Remember that God didn't tell Abraham where he was going to from the beginning. He told him to leave his father's house and go to a land that would be shown him. How was he going to identify the land? God appeared to him in verse 7 and told him, "this is the land!" in response to that appearance, Abraham raised an **altar** to the Lord who appeared to him. The altar raised here was a spiritual system that covenanted this new territory to the God he had met. This happened when he just arrived Canaan. Having confirmed the land, Abraham decided to pitch his tent between Bethel and Hai (also called Ai) where he decided to build another **altar**. This time, the altar was not just to mark his encounter with God, but to serve as a portal for continual fellowship with the God he had met. When he returned from Egypt, he came back and stayed in the same place where he had raised an altar.

Many years later, Abraham had long died. Jacob his grandson Jacob was traveling to Haran, to his uncle's house and then the night fell and he decided to sleep. He was not trying to pray, he was not trying to seek God and it happened that by divine orchestration, he found himself lying at the same spot where Abraham had raised an altar unto God. Suddenly, the Bible says that he had a dream and saw a ladder ascending from the earth to the heaven, angels ascending and descending.

That portal was not opened the day Jacob arrived there. From the day Abraham raised that altar, that spiritual gate was opened and angelic traffic had been going on. Many people had been passing there and probably passing the night there but nothing spectacular happened to them until the carrier of the covenant that Abraham enacted upon that altar came. The altar was a token of the covenant between Abraham and his seed. So you can arrive that place and lie down and not see anything but if you are a seed of Abraham you must see that portal. So the moment Jacob came to that place and lay down, suddenly the gates of Heaven were opened and there was Yahweh standing at the top of the ladder. He said, "I had a deal with Abraham in this place and there are certain things that we agreed upon. One of those things is that the land on which you lay, I will give it to you." Imagine if Abraham raised that altar unto a demon spirit, Jacob would have still interacted with the demon spirit because it was between Abraham and his seed.

Now Jacob from the place of that experience went to the house of Laban where he laboured for Leah for seven years, and then Rachel for another seven years, and then worked for Laban for another seven years. While he was labouring there, in Genesis 35, Jacob was dwelling around Shechem, the locality where Abraham built the first altar to signify his possession of the new land (Genesis 12:6) and because he understood that there was something about raising altars unto God, he raised (or rather reactivated) an altar in that place and God said, "No!, there is another altar that has been raised for our communion on your behalf, you don't need to raise another one. My dealings with you are based on the altar at Bethel. Rise up and go to Bethel and dwell there" (Gen 35:1). This was the same place Abraham dwelt (Genesis 12:8; 13:3).

Later Jacob left with his family, and came to Bethel. He activated that altar again and he called it El Bethel. Many years later, Israel came out of Egypt. They crossed the Jordan, brought down Jericho and wanted to fight a little city called Ai. Then a man called Achan took one of the accursed things and they couldn't defeat Ai. Joshua went to God and asked why they couldn't defeat Ai and God said that Israel had sinned. They cast lots and came to the point where they discovered who did it and cleansed the nation of that guilt. Before they went to war again, God gave them a strategy. The Bible said that they went to lay ambush at a particular spot and the spot where they laid ambush was between Bethel and Ai (Hai), the same place Abraham had dwelt. They never decided to go there but there was a force from the altar that was saying that, "This land has been given to Abraham and his seed. If you must take the land, you must align with the altar that Abraham had built." It was from that place that they began to defeat all the nations. Imagine the impact of one altar on many generations!

4. The influence of altar can only be broken via a legal court process

You don't wish your way out of the influence of an altar. The covenant of an altar is like the covenant of marriage. As long as marriage contract has been entered and consummated, the validity of that covenant can only come to an end either upon the death of a party to that marriage or through a legal court procedure for divorce. Even at that, Jesus tells us that court procedure does not dissolve marriage until a party dies. We discussed earlier that altars are trans-generational in their operation. They never die out with the person that erected them. Abraham had died but the altar was still alive even after many generations. It's amazing that many people are under the influence of one or more of these altars. There is however, an intelligence you must have to undo the effect of these altars. You don't just get delivered from an altar by saying, "I don't want your influence." That's not how marriage is broken. A wife does not tell the husband that she no longer wants the marriage. The marriage is still valid even though she is in her father's house because there is a legal process that brought the marriage so there must be a legal process that will end the marriage. You don't wish your way out of the influence of an altar. You don't. Brothers and Sisters, I am particularly interested in the negative altars. These negative altars have formed the foundations upon which our lives have been built.

Other things to note about Altars:

1. The kind of sacrifice upon an altar determines the power and potency of the voice of that altar.

2. The Spirit to whom an altar is raised determines the possibilities that the altar brings.

3. The removal of the physical monuments used to erect an altar does not end the speaking of that altar.

4. Altars are not just physical monuments, they can be people, institutions and territories.

5. Our possibilities in life are largely connected to the altars speaking over us, good or bad.

6. An altar's role can influence outcomes of in the lives of third parties or those who were not directly involved in the covenants.

The reason behind certain predicament, sicknesses and some of the trouble that we see in our lives, many of the failures that we experience is that there are altars that speak against us. Do you know that the effect of these altars become stronger with each passing generation? They become more destructive by the next generation so it will be unfair not to pay attention to the altars that are around our families and around the places where we come from. Altars are real and will stop you if you allow them.

Does it mean that the death of Jesus was in vain? No! The sacrifice of Jesus Christ is the reason we are having this discussion. Remember that the Lord is our judge, the Lord is our lawgiver, and the Lord is our King. Altars are real.

There are several ways that altars operate and affect people. In the next two chapters we will be looking at two of these systems through which altars influence people.

CHAPTER SEVEN

TERRITORIAL ALTARS AND FOUNDATIONS

There is a very interesting story in the book of Mark that clearly demonstrates the influence of territorial altars and foundations.

---

*22**When they arrived at Bethsaida**, some people brought a blind man to Jesus, and they begged him to touch the man and heal him. 23**Jesus took the blind man by the hand and led him out of the village**. Then, spitting on the man's eyes, he laid his hands on him and asked, "Can you see anything now?" 24The man looked around. "Yes," he said, "I see people, but I can't see them very clearly. They look like trees walking around." 25Then Jesus placed his hands on the man's eyes again, and his eyes were opened. His sight was completely restored, and he could see everything clearly. 26Jesus sent him away, saying, **"Don't go back into the village on your way home."***

Mark 8:22-26 NLT (Emphasis mine)

Jesus was at Bethsaida and they brought a blind man to him. Jesus held the hand of the blind man and took him out of the village before healing the man. The Bible didn't tell us why but I personally think that it may have to do with the territory. It may probably be that as long as the man was within that territory, Jesus, the son of God was limited in his ability to work miracles in the man's life. This may be the reason why Jesus had to warn the man not to go back to the village on his way home. Like I stated earlier, this is purely my personal opinion and does not form any theological position. If my opinion on this is true, does it mean that the moment they crossed the boundary, the forces of that territory could not exert any influence to prevent the man's healing anymore? My emphasis however is that we dwell in a legal realm and you must understand this to win.

There are possibilities that are seen in the lives of people merely coming from certain territories. You don't need to commit any sin as it were. You don't need to violate any law. The fact that you come from a particular place or dwell in a particular territory already implicates you.

Like we saw in the story of Abraham, the very first thing he did when he got to a new territory - Canaan - was to establish an altar unto a deity; God Almighty in this case. Similarly, there is no city, no hamlet, and no village whose first inhabitant did not enter a covenant with spirits before settling in. We can see this even in great nations like the United States of America where the founding fathers established the nation on covenants.

When you study the history of Nigeria and focus on the middle belt for instance, you will realize that there is a similarity in the spirits that operate within that region. Their predicaments are similar, their dimensions of witchcraft are similar and their limitations are similar. It is not necessarily what the people did; something was programmed into that territory that compels them to behave a certain way.

There is a region in Nigeria where the men demonstrate gross irresponsibility. The wives are often the bread winners of the families while the men just laze around. I have seen men from this region who were working and earning a living as singles but got married, and came under the influence of this territorial altar. The man stops working and the wife suddenly becomes the financial burden bearer and they don't see anything wrong about this.

You may not have chosen to come from such territories but that does not exonerate you from the impact of the altars that speak in that territory. Haven't you noticed that there are nations and cities in the scriptures that anytime God was declaring judgement on them; it was absolute? We often wonder what they did to have deserved such judgement. Let's take a quick look at a few examples:

1. Canaan

Canaan was the land that God told Israel to wipe out and not leave anybody alive. Why would God say to destroy Canaan? What did Canaan do? Idolatry? Are they the only ones who practiced idolatry? Israel was also involved in idolatry so why didn't God say to wipe them out? It was not about what the Canaanites did. A history pre-dated the inhabitants.

The Post Noah's Flood story...

The above scripture clearly states that the entire human race after the flood sprang up from Noah and his sons. Sometimes, we need to read between the lines and allow the Holy Spirit give us understanding of the mysteries that have been between those lines of scriptures.

It was obvious from the stories that followed that Ham had a behaviour that was different from that of his brothers, Shem and Japheth. How he got that behaviour, the Bible didn't say. Could it be that he had been interacting with the wicked people that God destroyed with the flood? The Bible didn't say but we would see that the evil and shameful behaviour of Ham as recorded in Genesis 9 was not consistent with the testimony of God for Noah that we saw in Genesis 6:9. One thing is certain, Ham had a faulty and questionable ideology on the basis of which he did what he did to his father.

I will not bore you with the theological debates as to what Ham did to his father exactly. It is however certain that whatever Ham did warranted a curse from his father and this curse was pronounced upon one of the sons of Ham called Canaan. The reason why it was Canaan that was cursed is still a subject of theological debate which I will not also bore you with. My point here is that Noah pronounced a curse upon Canaan and we would see that the curse manifest upon the territory that originated from this cursed man for many generations until Christ came.

Cities like Sidon, the city from where Jezebel, baal and ashtoreth originated (1 Kings 11:5; 16:31; 1 Chronicles 1:13), and Sodom and Gomorrah (Genesis 18:20-33) originated from this cursed son of Ham – Canaan. Their evil as we will later see in scripture predates them in as much as their personal will was involved. This was why God would give an instruction for outright annihilation of the people of Canaan because of their foundation and their evil manifestation at the time.

2. Babylon

How about Babylon? Even until the book of Revelation, Babylon was still being punished. What is the offence of Babylon? Is there something more than what we see on the surface? We will allow scriptures to answer these questions.

Babylon also originated from the same Ham but not through Canaan this time. You will recall that the behaviour of Ham after the flood did not exactly follow the pattern of his father's righteous living which exempted them from the flood judgement in the first place. It's therefore not surprising that we see various evil manifestations from his offspring, first the descendants of Canaan and now the descendants of Cush.

---

*6The sons of Ham were **Cush**, Mizraim, Put, and Canaan. 7The sons of Cush were Seba, Havilah, Sabtah, Raamah, and Sabtechah; and the sons of Raamah were Sheba and Dedan. 8Cush begot Nimrod; he began to*

<blockquote>
be a mighty one on the earth. ⁹He was a mighty hunter before the Lord; therefore it is said, "Like Nimrod the mighty hunter before the Lord." 10 And the beginning of his kingdom was Babel, Erech, Accad, and Calneh, in the land of Shinar. 11 From that land he went to Assyria and built Nineveh, Rehoboth Ir, Calah, ¹²and Resen between Nineveh and Calah (that is the principal city).

Genesis 10:6-12 (Emphasis mine)
</blockquote>

Cush was the firstborn of Ham. The Bible said that Cush gave birth to four sons and listed their names in Genesis 10: 8. The Bible went further to tell us that Cush gave birth to another son called Nimrod who was not listed among the sons in verse 8. The fact that this particular son was separated from the others calls for close investigation. I believe that there was something about this particular son that was worth studying. The Bible says that Cush begat Nimrod and he became a mighty one in the earth. What is the problem with becoming a mighty man in the earth? After all, it is the desire of everyone to be great you may say. The next statement is what is actually disturbing. *He was a mighty hunter before the Lord; therefore it is said,* **"Like Nimrod the mighty hunter before the Lord."** Nimrod was not only mighty, he was mighty in competition with God and His systems. Does that remind you of someone who was cast down from heaven (Isaiah 14:12-14)?

The Hebrew word *'Paniym'* translated *'before'* in verse 9 of Genesis 10 was also had other meanings like *'against'*, *'forefront' and 'more than'* amongst other meanings [1]. I personally don't think there is anything wrong with being a mighty man before God after all we are all before Him but I think there is everything wrong with being mighty in rebellious to God. The account of the rebellion he led in the proposed building of the tower of Babel makes me believe that Nimrod had become a standard of rebellion and wickedness at that time.

---

[1]Now the whole earth had one language and one speech. [2]And it came to pass, as they journeyed from the east, that they found a plain in the land of Shinar, and they dwelt there. [3]Then they said to one another, "Come, let us make bricks and bake them thoroughly." They had brick for stone, and they had asphalt for mortar. [4]And they said, "Come, let us build ourselves a city, and a tower whose top is in the heavens; let us make a name for ourselves, lest we be scattered abroad over the face of the whole earth."

Genesis 11:1-4

---

[1] (OT6440) BIBLESOFT'S NEW EXHAUSTIVE STRONG'S NUMBERS AND CONCORDANCE WITH EXPANDED GREEK-HEBREW DICTIONARY. Copyright © 1994, 2003, 2006 Biblesoft, Inc. and International Bible Translators, Inc. All rights reserved.

If we flip the pages back to Genesis 10:10, which was talking about Nimrod; still on territorial altars and foundations, we will then find out that the beginning of his kingdom was Babel. Wait a minute, Nimrod was a king? Who crowned him king? His might in rebellion rose to a point that he became a self-acclaimed king – the beginning of human government. Nimrod had built cities which began with Babel. It was within this Babel that he attempted to build a tower which God stopped by confusing their languages. Another interesting thing we see is that his kingdom was built in a mysterious land called Shinar. It will interest you to know that the land of Shinar is Babylon. So it was Nimrod that built Babylon!

---

*¹In the third year of the reign of Jehoiakim king of Judah, Nebuchadnezzar **king of Babylon** came to Jerusalem and besieged it. ²And the Lord gave Jehoiakim king of Judah into his hand, with some of the articles of the house of God, which he carried into **the land of Shinar to the house of his god**; and he brought the articles into the treasure house of his god.*

Daniel 1:1-2 *(Emphasis mine)*

The land of Shinar; the Babylonian system, became the base of wickedness in the earth.

Babylon was built upon the foundation of rebellion and
wickedness, an anti-Christ system established to draw men
away from God. As a result of this foundation, there was
nothing they could ever do to avert the judgement of God
upon them as a territory. They could as individuals through
the sacrifice of Jesus Christ. When you come into this
territory, suddenly the system begins to teach you the
language and tongue of the territory. They begin to feed you

with the delicacies of the system to contaminate the seed of God in you.

In the book of Revelation, Babylon was no longer just a territory, it had become a goddess – Mystery, Babylon, The mother of Harlots and of the Abominations of the earth.

---

³So he carried me away in the Spirit into the wilderness. And I saw a woman sitting on a scarlet beast which was full of names of blasphemy, having seven heads and ten horns. ⁴The woman was arrayed in purple and scarlet, and adorned with gold and precious stones and pearls, having in her hand a golden cup full of abominations and the filthiness of her fornication. ⁵And on her forehead a name was written: MYSTERY, BABYLON THE GREAT, THE MOTHER OF HARLOTS AND OF THE ABOMINATIONS OF THE EARTH.

Revelation 17:3-5

The Bible said that she caused the kings of the earth to commit harlotry. You are programmed to behave like her when you find yourself within her territory.

It was not a question of whether Babylonians hated Israel or not, they were eventually going to be destroyed no matter how good they were. The blood of Jesus can only save the individuals in it by personal exemption but the land itself has to perish because as far as God is concerned, the land stands as a rebellious antichrist system that must be destroyed. Why?

Because of the man that built it and the foundation upon which it was built!

3. Nineveh

What was Nineveh's offence? The Bible in the book of Jonah never told us what Nineveh did wrong.

---

¹Now the word of the Lord came to Jonah the son of Amittai, saying, ²"Arise, go to Nineveh, that great city, and cry out against it; for their wickedness has come up before Me."

Jonah 1:1-2

We just saw that God asked Jonah to get up and go and cry against Nineveh because their wickedness had come up before Him. What wickedness? We were not told. What did Jonah know about the wickedness of Nineveh that he didn't want to go and speak to them? Why was Jonah angry when God changed His mind about punishing Nineveh? There was something that Jonah knew about Nineveh that he thought qualified them for the destruction their repentance averted. Jonah was a prophet and his assignment was to speak the counsel of God. So, when he saw God forgiving the people of Nineveh, he said, "No! Based on what I have seen in the spirit, this city does not qualify to stay alive."

But the King and his men had exempted themselves. It looked as if God did not destroy Nineveh again but when you look at the book of Nahum, and Zephaniah, the judgement still happened. What was Nineveh's offence?

Nineveh, just like Babylon also originated from Ham, the son of Noah. In verse 11 of Genesis 10, the Bible says that Nimrod went to Assyria and there he built Nineveh. Who built Nineveh? So why did God say Nineveh should be destroyed? You answered correctly. Like Babylon it was a city built upon the foundation of rebellion and the antichrist system. The people of Nineveh who repented in sackcloth in the time of Jonah were able to exempt only themselves. They fasted and told God, "We have no part in this thing so we should not suffer for the things our fathers did." God said, "These people are sincere. I will still destroy this place but let me exempt this generation." This however did not stop the written judgement to be executed upon them later. You will notice that the judgement of God upon these territories was total annihilation of the inhabitants.

4. Edom

The nation of Edom is the nation born from the descendants of Esau.

----

³...I rejected... Esau, and devastated his hill country. I turned Esau's inheritance into a desert for jackals."⁴Esau's descendants in Edom may say, "We have been shattered, but we will

Malachi 1:3-4 *(NLT)*

How can God be forever angry with a people and will personally supervise to ensure that they fail as a nation? What did they ever do that cannot be atoned for? What was their offense? Are they not Abraham's descendant again?

We will explore the foundations of these nations from the word of God and see why God would give these final verdicts on them.

We've discussed extensively, the role of Nimrod Cush in the establishment of the antichrist systems. It was obvious he was under the influence of the spirit of the antichrist who was in search of the seed of the woman that God talked about in Genesis 3:15.

It more or less looked like Satan kept quiet after Nimrod for a while and was watching until Shem began to give birth to the point that he had a great grandson called Terah. Satan discovered that God entered a covenant with Terah's son – Abraham. Satan understood that the 'seed of the woman' he was seriously searching for would come from this covenant. How did he know this? He heard God mention seed when He was talking with Abraham.

I can imagine Satan asking himself; "Could this be the seed that God was talking about?" He began to follow that genealogy in search of the seed to see what he could do to avert the prophecy. Rebecca, the wife of Abraham's son – Isaac – had a challenge with conception for twenty years of marriage. When she got pregnant eventually after Isaac entreated the Lord for her, she noticed a serious and disturbing struggle in her womb. What did she do? She went to God and asked; "Why am I like this?" This was what God told her:

The children within her womb were not just two humans but two bodies housing two different spiritual systems seeking dominion in the earth. The contention of these systems began from the womb. I wouldn't want to be presumptive here with respect to who or what these systems are. One thing God stated clearly in the above scripture is that the system that is housed in the body of the younger shall be stronger than the older and shall be the one with the mandate for dominion.

I saw a very disturbing scripture in the book of Malachi.

*¹The burden of the word of the Lord to Israel by Malachi. ²"I have loved you," says the Lord. "Yet you say, 'In what way have You loved us?' Was not Esau Jacob's brother?" Says the Lord. "Yet **Jacob I have loved**; ³But **Esau I have hated**, and laid waste his mountains and his heritage or the jackals of the wilderness."*

Malachi 1:1-3

Why will God who is Love say that He hates a person He created and this, before they were born. What did Esau do? Was it Esau He hated? No! It was the spiritual system inside Esau that God hated. How did you know this Pastor Alfa, you may ask? Alright, let's see what the scripture has to say.

*So the boys grew. And **Esau was a skilful hunter**, a man of the field; but Jacob was a mild man, dwelling in tents.*

Genesis 25:27 *(Emphasis mine)*

The occupation the boys chose was indicative of the spiritual system they represented. Esau was a skilful hunter while Jacob was a shepherd. When the sons of Jacob would come to Egypt many years later, they told Pharaoh that being shepherds was an occupation of their tribe. This is because they were the generation that should bring forth the Christ, the good shepherd and so even their occupation had to align with that prophecy.

So how did Esau become a hunter? Who taught him? Let's rewind back to our previous discussion on Nimrod. Nimrod was the first person who was mentioned as a hunter in the Bible (Genesis 10:9) and the very next person was Esau. A hunter cannot be a type of Christ. A hunter kills while a shepherd makes alive. Jesus never called Himself a hunter, He was called the good Shepherd. Being a hunter aligns more with the character of Satan who comes to steal, kill and destroy, as such cannot be a chosen occupation of one who will bring forth the Christ. The antichrist system in Nimrod was still hovering the earth seeking a body that would continue its agenda.

When God, before whom all things lay bare, saw the spiritual system in the child who would be the firstborn (Esau), He said "I hate this spiritual system embodied in Esau." "If I allow Esau to carry the blessing, it means I will be putting the Christ in an antichrist system."

Imagine for a moment the desolation that would have befallen the Edomites, the sons of Esau. Imagine the limitations on their efforts no matter how hard they tried. Their fate was already concluded because of the foundation upon which they were born and built.

Time will not permit to mention nations like Moab and Amor who were all born out of the incestuous relationship between Lot and his daughters, after they escaped from Sodom and Gomorrah. We saw a Moabitess by the name Ruth exempting herself later in scripture but it didn't stop the manifestation of the foundations upon which they were built.

In the same way, we come from many territories in this country and around the world that are built upon ancient demonic foundations that are speaking against us. The majority of the people are Christians but the altars are still alive and are speaking. You are doing the best you can but there is a level you cannot go beyond as long as you are part of these territories. Territorial altars are mysteries that can produce realities in the lives of people. However, the case of any man who has surrendered to the Lordship of Christ should be different. We will see this as we continue.

CHAPTER EIGHT

ANCESTRAL ALTARS AND FOUNDATIONS

Our fathers sinned and are no more, and we bear their punishment.

Lamentations 5:7 (NIV)

Our ancestors sinned, but they have died - and we are suffering the punishment they deserved!

Lamentations 5:7 (NLT)

The second aspect I want to talk about is what I call the mystery of tribes and ancestry. As we can see from our previous discussions, the demonic foundations of territories began with individuals. While there are certain demonic possibilities that are prevalent over territories, there are some that can be enacted and will only influence certain families and tribes. The same way territories can be under the influence of certain covenants, there are individuals also that enter certain covenants that become a snare to their offspring. On the other hand, there are individuals who were under the influence of curses that also became a snare to the children. Let's look at a few examples.

1. Moses

The life of Moses is a classic example of how ancestral foundations can hinder a man from fulfilling destiny. God had sent Moses to bring His people out of their captivity in Egypt. Moses had done great exploit in Egypt to secure their release. The rod of Aaron had turned into a serpent that swallowed the ones of the magicians in Egypt. The ten plagues dealt a colossal blow to the gods of Egypt. The red sea was parted and the children of Israel under Moses' leadership had walked through it on dry ground. Korah, Dathan and Abiram spoke against Moses and the ground swallowed them up. Miriam, his elder sister had spoken against him and she became leprous. Moses was a man who did great wonders. Unfortunately, the same Moses couldn't make it to the land of promise. What happened?

---

*²Now there was no water for the congregation; so they gathered together against Moses and Aaron.⁶So Moses and Aaron went from the presence of the assembly to the door of the tabernacle of meeting, and they fell on their faces. And the glory of the Lord appeared to them. ⁷Then the Lord spoke to Moses, saying, ⁸"Take the rod; you and your brother Aaron gather the congregation together. **Speak to the rock***

***before their eyes**, and it will yield its water;*
thus you shall bring water for them out of
the rock, and give drink to the congregation
and their animals." ⁹So Moses took the rod
from before the Lord as He commanded him.
¹⁰And Moses and Aaron gathered the
assembly together before the rock; and he
said to them, **"Hear now, you rebels! Must**
we bring water for you out of this
rock?"¹¹Then **Moses lifted his hand and**
struck the rock twice with his rod; *and*
water came out abundantly, and the
congregation and their animals drank.
¹²Then the Lord spoke to Moses and Aaron,
"Because you did not believe Me, to
hallow Me in the eyes of the children of
Israel, therefore you shall not bring this
assembly into the land which I have
given them."

Numbers 20:2, 6-12 *(Emphasis mine)*

What really stopped Moses from entering the land of promise? God told Moses to speak to the rock and Moses, in anger, because of the murmurings of the people, struck the rock twice. There was a time they needed water that God asked Moses to strike the rock which he did and water came out. This second time, he was meant to speak to the rock but in anger he struck the rock twice. Even though it was bad enough that he disobeyed God's instructions, it was more grievous because that rock he was striking is Christ and

Christ was meant to suffer once. His striking the rock a second time as against speaking to the rock for water to come out was a violation of divine ordinance for which he was punished. God said, *Because you did not believe Me, to hallow Me in the eyes of the children of Israel, therefore you shall not bring this assembly into the land which I have given them.* But was it just anger? No! It was not just anger.

Recall that Moses was born at a time of serious turbulence such that he was placed by the Nile where Pharaoh's daughter picked and raised him. Satan had obviously been searching for how he can destroy the deliverer. He had seen Moses display anger several times. Satan probably discovered that there was something unique about Moses' anger. What was it?

The Bible tells us in Exodus 2:1 that a man of the house of Levi went and took as wife a daughter of Levi who conceived and gave birth to a son. That was how the story of Moses began, isn't it? This means both the father and mother of Moses were Levites.

Genesis 49:1 *says,*

...Jacob called his sons and said, "Gather together, that I may tell you what shall befall you in the last days...

Did Jacob say gather yourselves and your descendants together? Did he say, "My sons gather your wives and your families, let me tell them what will happen?" He said, "I am going to be speaking to you as individuals." In verse 2, he says *"Gather together and hear, you sons of Jacob, and listen to Israel your father."* Israel was the carrier of the Abrahamic covenant. Remember that the name, Israel was given to him after he encountered God at Peniel. So Jacob used that name as an indication of his office as the current bearer of the Abrahamic covenant. "In other words, what I am about to say will not fall to the ground."

In verse 5-7, Jacob continues,

Simeon and Levi are brothers; Instruments of cruelty are in their dwelling place. ⁶Let not my soul enter their council; Let not my honour be united to their assembly; for in their anger they slew a man, and in their self-will they hamstrung an ox. ⁷Cursed be their anger, for it is fierce; and their wrath, for it is cruel!

So before Moses was born, there was already a curse on his lineage. Even though the father of Moses was neither the direct son of Jacob nor the direct son of Levi, the curse still found expression in Moses. They probably might have forgotten this thing. It was Moses himself that wrote this. "Cursed be their anger." A curse is the opposite of a blessing. To bless means to empower to succeed, to curse means to empower to fail. "Empowered to bring failure be their anger," was what Jacob said in essence and years passed and the tribe of Levi were giving birth until Moses came on the scene. His encounter with God in the burning bush removed leprosy but did not remove this curse because it was factored in a nature that only the sacrifice of Jesus on the cross could take away. His dwelling in the presence of God for 40 days, to a point that his face was glowing, did not remove this curse. His encounter with God the second time did not remove this curse. His seeing the back of God did not remove this curse. He was going to the presence of God with a curse and coming out with a curse. Satan was not threatened by these encounters because there was something that he had studied. This man may have dutifully followed God, doing miracles in Egypt but one day...

And because Satan followed Moses, the first time he tried to destroy Moses was through pharaoh. It didn't work. So he said, 'Let me study him again.' And for forty years, he was studying until one day he saw that Moses in anger killed an Egyptian. Satan probably said, "This anger is not ordinary "and began to study until he saw that there was something Jacob placed upon the anger of Levi, from whose loins Moses came and said, 'Let me explore this.' He did it the first time when they served the golden calf. Moses was angry and he broke the commandments. God did not kill him; he melted the golden calf and gave them to drink. Satan said, 'We are getting close.' Until it came to the point where Moses struck the rock in anger and God prevented him from entering the land promise. I personally believe that the intensity of his loss on account of this curse was the reason why he had to make new pronouncements upon all the tribes in Deuteronomy 33.

2. David

Another person who falls under this category was David. David was the son of Jesse who was a descendant of Judah. If we must understand what is running in their tribe, then we have to look at the progenitor of the tribe himself. The story is found in Genesis 38.

Judah gave birth to three sons. The first one was wicked before God and God killed him. The second was wicked before God and God killed him. The third one was growing and Judah refused to give him to Tamar to marry as required by law. The Bible says that Tamar disguised herself as a harlot and Judah slept with her.

It appeared like it was a usual practice for Judah to patronize harlots. As far as Judah was concerned, he saw a harlot by the road and went to help himself but unfortunately, he didn't have money to pay so he dropped his sceptre, the symbol of his authority as collateral. After some days he sent his friend to collect the sceptre and deliver the price but the friend could not find the harlot. The Bible says that after some time Tamar became pregnant and according to the law, she was to be stoned because she had committed adultery. Then she brought out the sceptre and said, "The owner of this sceptre is responsible." So Judah got his son's wife pregnant! We can see where David got this from. It was a weakness strengthened by an ancestral foundation. Counselling will not solve this. The foundation has to be dealt with for freedom to happen.

David was the tenth generation from Judah.

*³Judah begot **Perez** and Zerah by Tamar,
Perez begot **Hezron**, and Hezron begot
Ram. ⁴Ram begot **Amminadab**, Amminadab
begot **Nahshon**, and Nahshon begot
Salmon. ⁵Salmon begot **Boaz** by Rahab,
Boaz begot **Obed** by Ruth, Obed begot **Jesse**,
⁶and Jesse begot **David** the king.*

Matthew 1:3-6

Meanwhile, Deuteronomy 23:2 (KJV) tells us that:

*A bastard shall not enter into the
congregation of the Lord; even to his tenth
generation shall he not enter into the
congregation of the Lord.*

The Hebrew word '*mamzer*' translated bastard means *a mongrel, i.e. one born of a Jewish father and a heathen mother*[2]. Tamar the mother of Pharez and Zerah was a Canaanite.

---

[2] (OT4464) BIBLESOFT'S NEW EXHAUSTIVE STRONG'S NUMBERS AND CONCORDANCE WITH EXPANDED GREEK-HEBREW DICTIONARY. Copyright © 1994, 2003, 2006 Biblesoft, Inc. and International Bible Translators, Inc. All rights reserved.

David's decent was from this family forbidden by law from entering into the congregation of the Lord. David however was exempted from this banishment as he himself was reckoned as a man after God's heart which is a pointer to what the grace of our Lord Jesus Christ has achieved for us. We will explore this in the subsequent chapters. This notwithstanding, David seemed to still be under the influence of this foundational spirit of immoral sexual relationship. Although he was loving God, achieving great feats like killing Goliath and bringing freedom to an entire nation, singing songs and writing psalms, this foundational spirit was still seeking to find expression in him. It was not afraid of his worship, it was not afraid of his singing to God. It kept following him until the day we saw its manifestation. I do not think that Bathsheba was the first married woman that David lusted after. The Bible says that when Nabal died, David went and married Abigail his widow. Logically thinking, at what point did David start nursing a desire for Abigail? When Nabal died? I don't think so. I believe he didn't carry out his desires when he first saw Abigail because he didn't have the power to do so since he wasn't on the throne yet. I also do not think that David was a morally depraved person that will just stand up and begin to lust after another man's wife. Remember that he was a man after God's heart. I believe it was a struggle with that foundational spirit of immorality.

3. The Descendants of King Saul

Another very interesting story that illustrates the operation of ancestral altars and foundations is found in the book of 2 Samuel 21:1-14. There was a very serious famine during the reign of David for about three years which was attributed to something Saul did while he was alive. Saul had slain the Gibeonites who were living among the Israelites. The Gibeonites deceived Joshua and the leaders of Israel into making a covenant with them. It was this covenant that Saul violated and the heavens were shut over God's own Israel.

When David consulted the Gibeonites to know what they would want as an atonement, they demanded that seven sons of the house of Saul be delivered to them to sacrifice to which David obliged.

7But the king spared Mephibosheth the son of Jonathan, the son of Saul, because of the Lord's oath that was between them, between David and Jonathan the son of Saul. 8So the king took Armoni and Mephibosheth, the two sons of Rizpah the daughter of Aiah, whom she bore to Saul, and the five sons of Michal the daughter of Saul, whom she brought up for Adriel the son of Barzillai the Meholathite; 9and he delivered them into the hands of the Gibeonites, and they hanged them on the hill before the Lord. So they fell, all seven together, and were put to death in the days of harvest, in the first days, in the beginning of barley harvest.

2 Samuel 21:7-9

Seven innocent men who had no hand in what Saul did paid with their lives and God watched with approval because he is a covenant keeping God. The only reason this people died was that they were descendants of Saul. We saw another covenant displayed when another covenant between David and Jonathan spared Mephibosheth, the son of Jonathan. As a grandson of Saul, he qualified to die but as a son of Jonathan, David's friend, he was exempted from the evil that came with the name of Saul. Like Mephibosheth, we can also be exempted because of Jesus. We discuss this as we continue.

4. Abiathar the Priest

God was angry with the house of Eli, the priest and had declared His judgement concerning their priesthood (1 Samuel 2:27-32; 3:12-14). God had changed His mind concerning the everlasting priesthood of the house of Eli because of the atrocities of his children that he didn't do anything about.

Abiathar the son of Ahimelech was the priest that served during the reign of David the King. Abiathar was a descendant of Eli. When David was very old and was about to die, Adonijah conferred with Joab, the commander of David's army and Abiathar, the priest to crown him as king in place of his father. The coup failed and Solomon was crowned king. As a punishment for his betrayal, Solomon removed him from being priest.

Solomon thought he was punishing Abiathar for his betrayal, little did he know that he was fulfilling a judgement that was hanging on his ancestry. That judgement was responsible for his actions in supporting Adonijah against David's choice of Solomon. People don't just misbehave. There are forces stronger than them that manipulates their actions to make the ground fertile for curses and judgements to find fulfilment. This does not in any way attribute all misbehaviours to spiritual forces alone even though there is a spirit at work in children of disobedience (Ephesians 2:2). The judgement that was declared at Shiloh was being fulfilled in Jerusalem after more than a hundred years.

Nothing just happens. Moses and David were men that represent a strange dimension in God. If they were not exempted, there must be something you must know that will set you free. Men don't just access freedom by desire, there must be something known and understood. Territories can bring someone under an influence, tribes can bring someone under an influence. But has God left us without hope? No. He hasn't. There is a bail - out plan. However, before I talk about the bail - out plan, we'll discuss how Satan explores the judicial system of God to destroy us.

PART THREE

THE COURT OF HEAVEN

CHAPTER NINE

THE ACCUSER OF THE BRETHREN

*Then I heard a loud voice saying in heaven,
"Now salvation, and strength, and the
kingdom of our God, and the power of His
Christ have come, for the accuser of our
brethren, who accused them before our God
day and night, has been cast down.*

Revelation 12:10

The undoing of many of us in the Body of Christ is that we have not paid close attention to the interplay of the Fatherhood of God and His system of divine justice. There is a system of divine justice established by God which we must understand and take advantage of so that we can appropriate the things that have been purchased for us by the Blood of the eternal covenant.

The scripture above is a proclamation that was made in heaven when the Michael-led team of angels banished Satan and his angels from heaven. Satan was called a very interesting name here – accuser of the brethren, which is actually the meaning of his name – Satan. The interesting thing is that he does this accusation day and night. So, Satan accuses our brethren to our Father who loves us and he does this day and night. How does he get God's attention? Is there something that grants him legal ground to approach God and even accuse His children to Him when he had been banished from heaven? Where does Satan do this accusation since he has been banished? Let's look at the story of Job.

---

¹There was a man in the land of Uz, whose name was Job; and that man was blameless and upright, and one who feared God and shunned evil... ⁶Now there was a day when the sons of God came to present themselves before the Lord, and Satan also came among them...⁸Then the Lord said to Satan, "Have you considered My servant Job, that there is none like him on the earth, a blameless and upright man, one who fears God and shuns evil?" ⁹So Satan answered the Lord and said, "Does Job fear God for nothing? ¹⁰Have You not made a hedge around him, around his household, and around all that he has on every side? You have blessed the work of his hands, and his possessions have increased in the land. ¹¹But now, stretch out Your hand and touch all that he has, and he will surely curse You to Your face!" ¹²And the Lord said to Satan, "Behold, all that he has is in your power; only do not lay a hand on his person." So Satan went out from the presence of the Lord.

Job 1:1, 6, 8-12

For Job, the story began by waking up one morning and bad news began to hit him from every corner. His seven sons and three daughters were kidnapped in one day (Job 1:13-15), he lost his great wealth in three disasters that all happened in one day (Job 1:16-19). As far Job was concerned, it was a very bad day, but that's not where the story started from. There was a part of the story that happened in another realm that Job wasn't privy to. There was a court session that took place and considered the case of Job. There was an accuser who brought accusations before the Judge of the universe and based on the strength of his case was able to secure a warrant to cross examine Job. Job wasn't privy to all of these. It was even God who presented a defence for Job. Why couldn't God shut Satan up when God Himself testified of Job's uprightness? When Satan requested for permission to strike job, why couldn't God veto it. When you look at the statement of God after the first attack, it is clear that He desired to prevent Job from being attacked by Satan but what made it difficult for God to stop Satan from attacking Job? Let's see how the justice system of God works.

I do not have a background in law but from my interaction with law professionals, I will briefly discuss a few terms that will help us understand the divine justice systems of God.

1. The judge:

A Judge is the person vested with the authority to hear, determine, and preside over legal matters brought in a court of law. God Almighty is Judge of the heavenly court (Isaiah 33:22; Genesis 18:25).

2. The Prosecutor:

The prosecution is the legal party responsible for presenting the case in a criminal trial against an individual accused of breaking the law. The legal representative of the prosecution is the prosecutor. The prosecutor often represents a government in the case brought against the accused person. In a criminal procedure, it is the responsibility of the prosecution to prove that the defendant is guilty beyond any reasonable doubt[3].

Satan is the prosecutor in our case who brings accusations before God the Judge and he often makes effort to convince the Judge that we are guilty of his accusations. Why does he do this? Is he not aware of the implications of the cross of Jesus? Doesn't he know that every handwriting of ordinances that was contrary to us has been blotted out? He sure knows. Satan often tries his luck to see whether the ignorance of believers will open a window for him to wreck needless assaults. It is his right to be heard in the heavenly court and he explores that right very well. He accuses our brethren day and night!

Remember the story of Job? Satan came to God bringing accusations against Job. But Satan has been cast down (Revelation 12:10). Where did this conversation happening

---

[3] https://en.wikipedia.org/wiki/Prosecutor

since he had been banished from heaven? He met God in court.

Let me give a simple illustration. Assuming that a lawyer was working with a chamber and was fired for misbehaving. Years later the principal of the chamber was appointed as a high court judge. If this young lawyer has a case to defend before his former boss, will he be prevented from coming to the court because of the personal issues they had? I don't think so. It is on this ground that Satan can still appear before God to bring accusations against God's people. For instance, he comes before God with an accusation that a particular person is from this territory and based on the records, these are the things written about that territory and because of this, he cannot progress. This is where our fathers missed it!

3. The Defendant:

A defendant is a person accused of committing a crime in criminal prosecution or a person against whom some type of civil relief is being sought in a civil case (Wikipedia). In the story of Job that we mentioned earlier, Job was the defendant even though he never knew he was undergoing a court procedure. Whenever Satan brings an accusation against a person, that person becomes a defendant with respect to the matter in contention. For instance, we spoke about territorial and ancestral altars and foundations earlier. Satan often tries to bring accusations to God about such covenants in the biological genealogy of people even though he knows they are born again and have become new creatures. God is not unaware that you are longer under the influence of such altars and foundations but He must be just in His judgement. So He allows Satan exercise his right by bringing his accusation against you. You don't have to be guilty to be accused. Every accused person has the right to defend himself. The case however cannot end with just accusation. There is another party in court that we have to discuss too. That party is the Defense attorney.

4. Defense Attorney or Defense Counsel:

The Defense Attorney or Defense Counsel is a lawyer who represents a person accused of committing a crime. I came across a very interesting statement by the United States of America's Supreme Court:

---

*Even the intelligent and educated layman
has small and sometimes no skill in the
science of law. If charged with crime, he is
incapable, generally, of determining for
himself whether the indictment is good or
bad. He is unfamiliar with the rules of
evidence. Left without the aid of counsel he
may be put on trial without a proper charge,
and convicted upon incompetent evidence,
or evidence irrelevant to the issue or
otherwise inadmissible. He lacks both the
skill and knowledge adequately to prepare
his defense, even though he has a perfect
one. He requires the guiding hand of counsel
at every step in the proceedings against him.*

The most interesting part of this statement for me is that without a Defense Attorney or Counsel, an accused person may be convicted of a crime he is not guilty of because of his inability to establish his innocence.

As believers against whom Satan consistently brings accusations to prevent us from walking in the reality of our new life in Christ, we need the service of an Attorney who can stand in our defense in the heavenly Court. Thanks be to God that we have one.

[1]My dear children, I write this to you so that
you will not sin. But if anybody does sin, we
have one who speaks to the Father in our
defense — Jesus Christ, the Righteous One.
[2]He is the atoning sacrifice for our sins, and

[4] *https://www.nacdl.org/Article/June2012-TheRoleofDefenseCounselinEnsur*

1 John 2:1-2 (NIV)

Jesus Christ is our Defense Counsel. Hallelujah! Jesus is not only our redeeming, He is our legal representation in the heavenly court. In the case of Job, we never saw anyone in that assembly rising to the defense of Job but glory be to God we have our Lord and Saviour Jesus Christ is ever present with the Father to speak in our defense. Another scripture that buttresses this is in the book of Hebrews.

---

*...to God the Judge of all, to the spirits of just
men made perfect, 24 to Jesus the Mediator
of the new covenant...*

Hebrews 12:23-24

Jesus Christ is our Defense and His defense is based on the new covenant in His Blood, the same blood that declared us not guilty.

---

*33Who shall bring a charge against God's
elect? It is God who justifies. 34Who is he who
condemns? It is Christ who died, and
furthermore is also risen, who is even at the*

It's important we understand how both the prosecutor and the defense present their cases. How does Jesus advocate for us?

5. Judgement:

A judgement, in all legal systems refers to a decision of a court adjudicating the rights of the parties to a legal action before it. In other words, it is the responsibility of the judge to declare his judgement based on the evidence before him. He will either convict or acquit the accused person. The judge uses an invisible case to weigh the evidences before on the basis of which he makes his judgement. The two parties are expected to bring witnesses and tender their evidence in defense of their case. We will look at this two terms quickly.

Wikipedia defines a witness as someone who has knowledge about a matter. In a legal context, a witness is someone who, either voluntarily or under compulsion, provides testimonial evidence, either oral or written, of what he or she knows or claims to know. An evidence on the other hand, is anything presented in support of an assertion which may be strong or weak. The strongest type of evidence is that which provides direct proof of the truth of an assertion (Wikipedia).

The strength of any defense therefore is determined by the witnesses and the evidence tendered. Do we have witnesses? Of course, yes! We will look at this in the next chapter.

CHAPTER TEN

THE THREE THAT BEAR WITNESS IN EARTH

Our fathers were born in families that were under the influence of either territorial curses or ancestral curses. Then they met the missionaries who preached the Gospel to them and told them, "Give your lives to Christ and be saved." They sincerely gave their lives to Christ and they were genuinely saved but they didn't understand the difference between prophetic realities and the experience of it. I usually give this example:

Let's assume that my late father left me a parcel of land and gave me the documents to that land. That I possess those documents does not mean that someone cannot just wake up one day and say it's his land. I can pass by the land one day and see another person already attempting to raise a structure on a land that is legally mine. I cannot just confront such persons on the spot. Rather, I will take my proof of ownership to a court of competent jurisdiction and tell them that someone is trespassing on my land. The court will then summon the person and ask the person to present the evidence that shows the land belongs to him. The court will then weigh both evidence and say, "Based on the evidences before us, Meshach Alfa owns this land." Now the court will empower what we call the law enforcement agents so that anytime the man is found on the land again, I won't be the one to chase him off my property, there is an authority and power that will chase him.

So also, when we give our lives to Christ, get the certificate of birth and evidence of our inheritance, Satan still moves about our land. Unfortunately, all the average believer tries is to say "Get out!" You think he will go? No. It is only a court process that will give you the justice.

Claiming Your Inheritance: The Record and the Witnesses

Like I mentioned in my example of the land my father gave me, the court will require that I present the evidence that support my claims. Do we have a witness as believers? Let's look at the word of God.

---

*⁷For there are three that bear record in heaven, the Father, the Word, and the Holy Ghost: and these three are one. ⁸And **there are three that bear witness in earth, the spirit, and the water, and the blood:** and these three agree in one.*

1 John 5:7-8 (KJV – Emphasis mine)

We see in the scripture above that the heavenly judicial system is influenced by the record in heaven and the witness in earth. What exactly is the record in heaven? We will find the answer in 1 John 5:11.

And this is the record that God hath given to us eternal life, and this life is in his Son (KJV).

This record is very clear. The record stipulates that eternal life is only possible through Jesus Christ the Son of the living God. The record states that *there is no other name under heaven given among men by which we must be saved* (Acts 4:12). When Satan comes to the Father with his accusations, the perspective of the Father will not differ from that of the Word or the Holy Spirit because they are One. Satan's accusation is also based on this record. For instance, it is in the record that *the soul that sins shall die* (Ezekiel 18:4) and that *the wages of sin is death* (Romans 6:23). This part of the record is the emphasis of Satan but he forgot that the same record also states that *the gift of God is eternal life in Christ Jesus our Lord* (Romans 6:23b). The part of the record he doesn't know is that justice (truth) and mercy met themselves at the cross of Calvary (Psalm 85:10). The cross was a perfect demonstration of the wrath and the mercy of God. The cross of Jesus was the full demonstration of the judgement of God on man and the same cross was the demonstration of the mercy of God upon man. So while it is true based on the record that *all have sinned and have fallen short of the glory of God*, it is also in the record that we have been *justified freely by His grace through the redemption that is in Christ Jesus, whom God set forth as a propitiation by His blood, through faith, to demonstrate His righteousness, because in His forbearance God had passed over the sins that were previously committed, to demonstrate at the present time His righteousness, that He might be just and the justifier of the one who has faith in Jesus (Romans 3:23-26).*

This record however is in heaven, so it is the responsibility of the witnesses therefore to validate heaven's record in the earth. The three witnesses are the Spirit, the Water and the Blood.

1. The Witness of the Blood

---

*And they overcame him by the blood of the
Lamb and by the word of their testimony,
and they did not love their lives to the death.*

Revelation 12:11

John said, "They overcame him by the blood of the Lamb and the words of their testimonies for they loved not their lives even unto death." How did this overcoming happen experientially?

Revelations 5, John the beloved had been weeping because there was no one in heaven, on earth and beneath the earth who could take the book or break the seals thereof. But then one of the twenty four elders came to him and said, "Weep no more. For the Lion of the tribe of Judah has prevailed." The moment the elder said that, the others began to sing. What was the song?

The blood that Jesus shed on the cross was a transaction. He purchased us to God with His blood. He purchased us to God from every tribe, language, people and nation! Hallelujah!

The possibilities of a certain tongue, tribe or people should not have influence on you anymore. There was a payment made to purchase you from that tribe. There was a demand by the altars and foundations of that tribe, clan and nation which the blood paid in full. So if they are still asking for another payment, you can go to court. How can I pay you for a land and you still tell me the land belongs to you? The blood purchased men to God from every tribe and language and people and nation. Nation talks about territories. This is what the blood of Jesus did – it purchased men. This is the record. How does the blood validate this in the court session?

It is the battle of bloods at the court room. The blood is alive and can speak. There is a blood speaking against you and there is a blood speaking in your favour. The blood of Jesus speaks better things. The blood of Jesus speaks mercy. The blood of Jesus is an evidence that you have been punished for that crime already. It is like the blood of the Passover lamb in Egypt that was on the door post and lintels of houses. The presence of the blood was proof that death had happened in that house already. So when Satan says, "the soul that sinneth shall die", the blood of Jesus says, "death has already happened and affliction shall not arise a second time."

You will notice that the Bible did not say that the blood of sprinkling shuts the voice of the blood of Abel. This means that the blood of Abel still speaks but the better things spoken by the blood of Jesus are strong enough evidence that the price has been paid in full.

So the question is this: if this is true, why have I not seen it's reality in my life? It's one thing to proclaim freedom for the captives and another thing entirely to release the prisoners (Isaiah 61:1 – NIV).

The price has been fully paid, the freedom has been proclaimed, but the prisoners are yet to walk out of the prison. It takes more than the witness of the blood to walk in full dominion and victory. Why?

Let's look at the second witness.

2. The Witness of the Water

What is the witness of the Water saying? What is his testimony in court? Remember that the witnesses have to agree as one before their witness is accepted.

*26...that He (Christ) might sanctify and cleanse her **with the washing of water by the word,***27*that He might present her to Himself a glorious church, not having spot or wrinkle or any such thing, but that she should be holy and without blemish.*

Ephesians 5:26-27

The witness of the Water is the continuous cleansing ministry of the Word of God. Jesus said to His disciples in John 15:3, *"You are already clean because of the word which I have spoken to you."*

The purpose of this cleansing dimension of the Word of God is to take away every spot, wrinkle or blemish. It is our responsibility as believers to consistently present ourselves for the cleansing ministry of the word of God. Paul admonishes us to let the word of Christ dwell in us richly (Colossians 3:16).

The water dimension of the word of God sanctifies, it does not condemn. So, while the Blood declares your redemption, Water declares your sanctification. The Water is declaring your reality from the perspective of the new life in Christ Jesus. It is the Water that declares that if any man is in Christ, He is a new creature, old things are passed away, all things have become new (2 Corinthian 5:17). The Bible says that the purpose of this cleansing and sanctification is that Jesus who has the power to condemn, might present you to Himself blameless. If you are blameless before Him who has the power to condemn you, who else will condemn you? The challenge however, is that the word must find His way into your spirit for His voice to be activated.

Your words were found, and I ate them, and
Your word was to me the joy and rejoicing of
my heart

Jeremiah 15:16

It is this dimension that builds capacity in you to obtain your inheritance. Remember that the judge is governed by law.

So now, brethren, I commend you to God and
to the word of His grace, which is able to

build you up and give you an inheritance
among all those who are sanctified.

Acts 20:32

The fullness of the Word of God in your spirit is needed for the voice of the third witness to be effective.

3. The Witness of the Spirit

And I will ask the Father, and He will give you
another Comforter (Counselor, Helper,
*Intercessor, **Advocate**, Strengthener, and*
Standby), that He may remain with you forever

John 14:16 (AMP)

One of the ministries of the Holy Spirit to a believer is that He is our Advocate. But Jesus is our Advocate you may say. You are very correct. We shall see the advocacy of the Holy Spirit as we continue. Before that, let's quickly look at two strategic ministries of the Holy Spirit to a believer.

a. The Holy Spirit is the authentication of our redemption.

The Bible tells us that when we got born again, we were sealed with the Holy Spirit of promise (Ephesians 1:13; 4:30) and this seal is eternally inseparable as long as we are in

Christ. His assignment is to help us conform to the person of the Christ.

b. The Holy Spirit gives us utterance when we pray.

The Holy Spirit who bears the record in heaven is also a witness that stands in your defense. You will recall that when we were discussing the unique creation of man and the origin of altars, we did say that man requires the partnership of a spirit to access realities in the realm of the spirit. The court process happens in the realm of the spirit, so man needs the assistance of the Holy Spirit in order to participate in the court proceedings. How does this partnership happen?

The Spirit is an acceptable witness in the court of heaven when it comes to the matters of the earth. So in partnership with the Holy Spirit, man is able to be present in court to give his testimony. Jesus told the disciples in Acts 1:8 (Paraphrased), "But ye shall receive power after that the same Spirit who is an accredited witness comes upon you and you shall be witnesses unto me..." Your partnership with the Holy Spirit turns you into an accredited witness who can give valid testimony in the matters of the earth. So unlike Job, you won't be absent when your case is being decided. If they are discussing your job, you will be there, if they are discussing your progress, you will be present because in partnership with the Holy Spirit, you become an accredited witness. Hear what The Bible says about this in Isaiah 59:19b:

> *When the enemy comes in like a flood, the Spirit of the Lord will lift up a standard against him.*

So when Satan comes against you with his flood of accusations based on your past, ancestral altars and foundations, the Spirit of the Lord who now lives inside you will lift a standard of the word of God against him. While the testimony of the Blood will say, "I was the price that was paid for his redemption", the testimony of the Water will say, "I sanctified him and I've taken away every blemish from him!" Satan will ask for his right to cross examine you which he will not be denied. Remember that it is the responsibility of the prosecutor to prove beyond reasonable doubt that the accused person is guilty as charged. Jesus, your Defense Counsel raises an objection to the cross–examination but the just Judge will overrule the objection and allow the cross - examination to go on. He says, "According to divine justice, it is the right of the prosecution to cross – examine the defendant. Let the cross - examination go on. So, satan goes ahead to cross-examine you. This was what happened in the case of Job. Satan sought for permission to cross – examine Job and it was granted him.

11But now, stretch out Your hand and touch
all that he has, and he will surely curse You
to Your face!" 12And the Lord said to Satan,
"Behold, all that he has is in your power;
only do not lay a hand on his person"...

Job 1:11-12

4So Satan answered the Lord and said, "Skin
for skin! Yes, all that a man has he will give
for his life. 5But stretch out Your hand now,

Job 2:4-6

Your cross - examination begins with all manner of troubles. Suddenly everybody starts provoking you. You enter a business, no sales. Suddenly bad news is hitting you from every corner. Like Job, terrible things begin to happen to you without notice. The goal in Job's case was not to take away his resources or to inflict pain on his body, but to put him under pressure to curse God with his mouth. This is Satan's goal with you too. The Blood has spoken, the Water has spoken and you in partnership with the Holy Spirit is being cross-examined. Satan wants you to counter the speaking of the Blood. Satan knows that he cannot stop us but he believes he can pressure us to stop ourselves by making us counter the speaking of the Blood. Hear what Hebrews says:

---

*²⁴...and to the blood of sprinkling that speaks better things than that of Abel. Hear the Heavenly Voice ²⁵**See that you do not refuse Him who speaks**. For if they did not escape who refused Him who spoke on earth, much more shall we not escape if we turn away from Him who speaks from heaven...*

Hebrews 12:24-25 *(Emphasis mine)*

You accept what the Blood speaks by repeating what He is saying notwithstanding your present realities. This is where the challenge is but there is hope.

26Likewise the Spirit also helps in our weaknesses. For we do not know what we should pray for as we ought, but the Spirit Himself makes intercession for us with groanings which cannot be uttered. 27Now He who searches the hearts knows what the mind of the Spirit is, because He makes intercession for the saints according to the will of God. 28And we know that all things work together for good to those who love God, to those who are the called according to His purpose.

Romans 8:26-29

The Spirit helps our inability to align completely with the speaking of the Blood. He does this by making intercessions for us with groaning which cannot be uttered.

While the cross – examination is still going on, the Holy Spirit the Advocate is with you on earth and dwells inside of you while Jesus the Advocate is with the Father right in Court. The Spirit knows the mind of God, He knows exactly what you are expected to say or do to pass the cross - examination. He taps you in the night and says, "Don't sleep. Begin to pray in tongues." Sometimes you say that you are tired but He insists because He knows your matter is still being decided upon. Other times quickens other people to raise an altar of intercession on your behalf. After a while, He might say "Begin to rejoice, what is required at this point is praise for with joy you must draw from this well of salvation." At such times, the spiritual activities might not make sense because there is a partnership with the Holy Spirit in heaven and He's with you on earth.

But then you wake up in the morning and good news start hitting you on every side. You are wondering what you did but remember you were present in court.

That's not all, there are times that the Holy Spirit will edit your prayers and your words before they get to the Judge. He does that because what you may be asking for may not be what is in the will for you at the moment. So you are asking for an intervention and the Holy Spirit is asking the Father to give you more grace to wait a little longer because of the timing of the breakthrough. So as the scripture says; we know that all things, good or bad, work together for our good because the One who knows the things of God edited our Prayers to be in sync with the will of God. So like Paul, you rejoice in tribulations because you know that it will work a far exceeding weight of glory for you.

Like Job, when Satan is done with all his cross-examinations, the Bible will testify that you did not sin against God with your mouth. You passed the test, therefore the case is decided in your favour.

The question you may want to ask is this, "what if Satan is able to convince God that I am guilty?" God knows that there is no level of accusation or cross-examination that can invalidate the record of the cross. The salvation that came through the cross is absolute. Jesus himself is the author of eternal salvation to all those who obey him (Hebrews 5:9). He is confident in the testimony of the blood, the water and the Spirit that lives inside you. So He is not afraid to allow Satan test you knowing that the end of that trial will be to your elevation. Let's not forget that the Father had committed all judgements to the Son (John 5:22). If Jesus your Saviour who is also your Advocate with the Father is also the one judging in your matter, how can you lose? It is absolutely impossible. While Satan's goal for the cross-examination is to prove that you are guilty, God allows the cross-examination because of the lifting that will follow.

I made up my mind that I will never be absent when my matter is discussed in the heavenly court. I will so explore my partnership with Holy Spirit who lives inside of me to be present in the heavenly deliberation of the matters that concern my destiny. And this is my final invitation to you as well. Satan has been the one initiating the court process. He has been the one reporting. Not anymore. Take the matter to court. Let us pray!

Prayers and Declarations!

1. Lord, I thank you for the light I have received through this book. I thank you because the light I have received has broken the power of darkness over my life in the name of Jesus.

2. By the light I have received, let every secret operation of Satan in matters of my life and destiny be exposed in the name of Jesus.

3. I declare that I am a new creation in Christ Jesus. It is therefore illegal for any possibility orchestrated by ancestral or territorial foundations to find expression in my life. Every door that my ignorance has opened for the oppression in my life is closed in the name of Jesus.

4. I demand full restoration of everything I have lost by reason of my ignorance of the reality of my new life in Christ in Jesus name.

5. By the witness of the Spirit, the Water and the Blood, I shut the mouth of the accuser over my life in Jesus' name.

Final Declaration!

It is written, God has given me eternal life in His Son Jesus Christ. It is also written, there are three that bear witness in earth, the Spirit; the Water and the Blood... I declare that the Blood of Jesus has purchased me from every connection to an earthly tribe, language, people, country and any other human affiliation. I may be in the world but I am no longer of the world. I have been translated into the kingdom of God's dear Son. Every altar or foundation, whether ancestral or territorial claiming a hold on me does it illegally. I therefore demand that any blessing that have been hindered from coming to me on account of their claims be released right now in the name of Jesus.

www.ingramcontent.com/pod-product-compliance
Lightning Source LLC
Chambersburg PA
CBHW020529160726